AMS SYSTEM

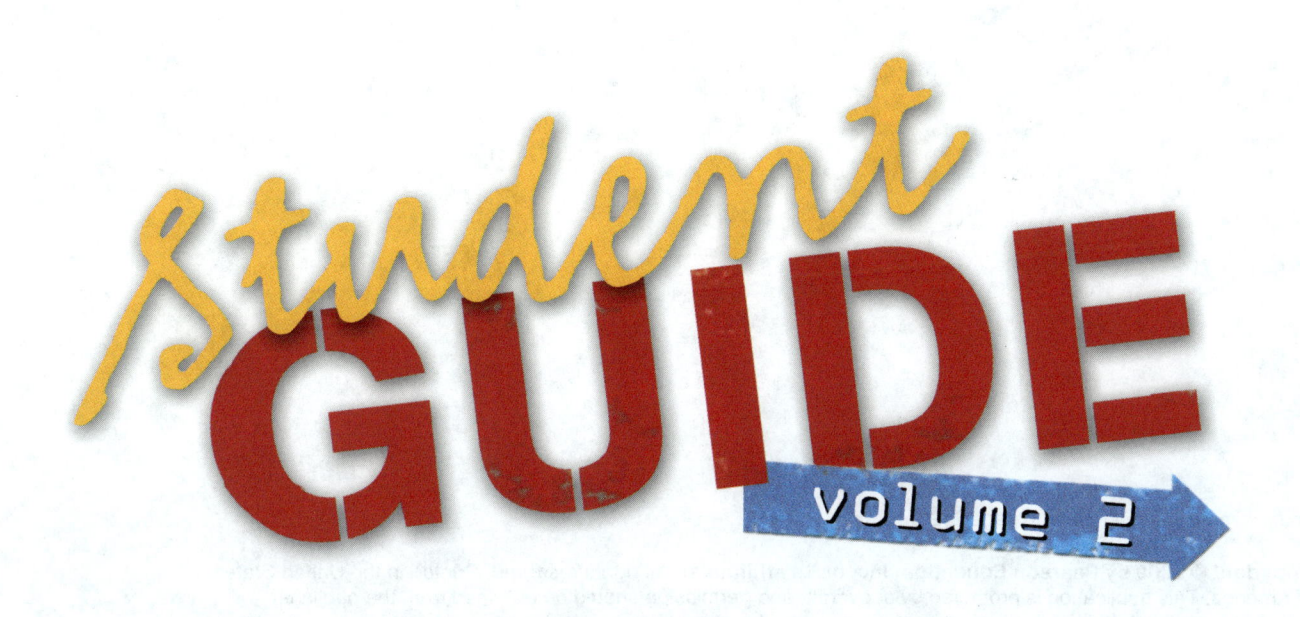

Student GUIDE
volume 2

Program Consultant
William F. Tate
Edward Mallinckrodt Distinguished University Professor
Washington University, St. Louis

PEARSON

Image credits can be found on page 242.

Copyright © 2009 by Pearson Education, Inc. or its affiliate(s). All rights reserved. Printed in the United States of America. This publication is protected by copyright, and permission should be obtained from the publisher prior to any prohibited reproductions, storage in a retrieval system, or transmission in any form or by any means, electronic, mechanical, photocopying, recording, or likewise. For information regarding permission(s), write to: Pearson School Rights & Permissions Department, One Lake Street, Upper Saddle River, New Jersey 07458.

Pearson® is a trademark, in the U.S. and/or in other countries, of Pearson Education, Inc. or its affiliate(s).

ISBN-13: 978-0-7854-6591-1
ISBN-10: 0-7854-6591-X
1 2 3 4 5 6 7 8 9 10 12 11 10 09 08

PEARSON

1-800-992-0244
www.pearson.com

CONTENTS

UNIT 5

Quick Recall and Fluency with Multiplication and Division

READING STRATEGY	Text Structure	2
LESSON 1	Learn the Skill	4
	Quick Recall of Basic Multiplication Facts	
LESSON 2	Choose a Strategy	7
LESSON 3	Learn the Skill	11
	Quick Recall of Basic Division Facts	
LESSON 4	Choose a Strategy	14
LESSON 5	Application	18
LESSON 6	Learn the Skill	22
	Multiplying Multidigit Numbers Using Models	
LESSON 7	Choose the Strategy	25
LESSON 8	Application	29
LESSON 9	Connections	33
	Finding Rules for Sequences of Numbers	
LESSON 10	Review and Practice	37
LESSON 11	Learn the Skill	41
	Multiplying Multidigit Numbers Using the Algorithm	
LESSON 12	Choose a Strategy	44
LESSON 13	Learn the Skill	48
	Mental Calculation	
LESSON 14	Choose a Strategy	51
LESSON 15	Application	55
LESSON 16	Learn the Skill	59
	Exponents	
LESSON 17	Choose a Strategy	62
LESSON 18	Application	66
LESSON 19	Connections	70
	Using Models to Represent Multidigit Division	
LESSON 20	Review and Practice	74
UNIT 5 REFLECTION		78

UNIT 6

Two-Dimensional Shapes

READING STRATEGY	Visualizing	80
USE THE STRATEGIES		82
LESSON 1	Learn the Skill	84
	Two-Dimensional Shapes	
LESSON 2	Choose a Strategy	87
LESSON 3	Learn the Skill	91
	Angles	
LESSON 4	Choose a Strategy	94
LESSON 5	Application	98
LESSON 6	Learn the Skill	102
	Describing and Classifying Shapes Using Sides and Angles	
LESSON 7	Choose a Strategy	105
LESSON 8	Application	109
LESSON 9	Connections	113
	Why Certain Shapes Are Not Polygons	
LESSON 10	Review and Practice	117
LESSON 11	Learn the Skill	121
	Decomposing, Combining, and Transforming Polygons	
LESSON 12	Choose a Strategy	124
LESSON 13	Learn the Skill	128
	Building, Drawing, and Analyzing Two-Dimensional Shapes	

(Contents continues)

UNIT 6 Two-Dimensional Shapes continued

LESSON 14	Choose a Strategy	131
LESSON 15	Application	135
LESSON 16	Learn the Skill	139
	Congruence and Symmetry	
LESSON 17	Choose a Strategy	142
LESSON 18	Application	146
LESSON 19	Connections	150
	Defining Two-Dimensional Space	
LESSON 20	Review and Practice	154
UNIT 6 REFLECTION		158

UNIT 7

Area of Two-Dimensional Shapes

READING STRATEGY	Metacognition	160
USE THE STRATEGIES		162
LESSON 1	Learn the Skill	164
	Area	
LESSON 2	Choose a Strategy	167
LESSON 3	Learn the Skill	171
	Area Units	
LESSON 4	Choose a Strategy	174
LESSON 5	Application	178
LESSON 6	Learn the Skill	182
	Using the Area Model	
LESSON 7	Choose a Strategy	185
LESSON 8	Application	189
LESSON 9	Connections	193
	Using Coordinate Grids to Find Area	
LESSON 10	Review and Practice	197
LESSON 11	Learn the Skill	201
	Estimating Area	
LESSON 12	Choose a Strategy	204
LESSON 13	Learn the Skill	208
	Decomposing Shapes to Find Area	
LESSON 14	Choose a Strategy	211
LESSON 15	Application	215
LESSON 16	Learn the Skill	219
	Using Symmetry and Congruence to Understand Transformations	
LESSON 17	Choose a Strategy	222
LESSON 18	Application	226
LESSON 19	Connections	230
	Justifying the Formula for the Area of a Rectangle	
LESSON 20	Review and Practice	234
UNIT 7 REFLECTION		238

Glossary 239

UNIT 5
Quick Recall and Fluency with Multiplication and Division

MATH SKILLS & STRATEGIES
After you learn the basic **SKILLS**, the real test is knowing when to use each **STRATEGY**.

READING STRATEGY
Learn to improve comprehension using Text Structure.

AMP LINK MAGAZINE
You Do the Math and Math Projects: After you read each magazine article, apply what you know in real-world problems.
Fluency: Make your reading smooth and accurate, one tip at a time.

CONNECTIONS
You own the math when you make your own connections.

VOCABULARY
MATH WORDS:
Know them!
Use them!
Learn all about them!

Reading Comprehension Strategy

Reading Comprehension Strategy: Text Structure

How to Use Text Structure

Preview the text to get an idea of its organization and purpose.

Identify the text structure. Use clues and signal words to identify problem and solution, description, sequence, cause and effect, and compare and contrast.

In some writing, you will have to **identify multiple structures** in text.

Summarize text by thinking about its structure.

All writing is organized, or structured, in a way that serves a purpose. This is the text structure. Preview the article by reading the title and subtitles. What do they tell you about the article's purpose and organization?

Hybrid Cars: The Answer to Air Pollution in Cities?

Hybrid cars are often in the news these days. People want to know, "Should I buy a hybrid car? Will it help the air stay cleaner?" To answer these questions, people must know what hybrid cars are and how they work.

1. What do the title and subtitles tell you about the subject of the article?

   thay will be talking about hybrid cars and how thay work

There are five kinds of text structure. *Problem and solution* describes a problem and its solution. *Description* helps the reader understand how someone or something looks, acts, works, feels, or thinks. *Sequence* explains the order of certain events. *Cause and effect* tells what happened and why. *Compare and contrast* shows how things are alike and different.

Gasoline Cars and Electric Cars

Most cars run on gasoline. Fuel is burned up as it is used. This burning fuel causes pollution. Electric cars, on the other hand, run on batteries. When the batteries are empty, the cars stop running. The batteries need to be charged. This makes it hard to plan long drives.

Electric cars run on batteries rather than gasoline.

2. What signal words and phrases do you see in this passage? What kind of text structure do they indicate?

   on the other hand it's comparing and contrasing.

Each kind of structure has its own signal words and phrases.

Structure	Signal Words
Problem and solution:	if/then, therefore, the problem is, the question is, one solution is
Description:	descriptive words or phrases
Sequence:	first, then, next, before, afterward
Cause and effect:	because, so, since, as a result
Compare and contrast:	alike, same, similarly, both, different, however, instead, but

Reading Comprehension Strategy

Hybrid Cars—A Bit of Both

A hybrid car uses both gasoline and a battery to power its engine. It puts out less pollution than a gas engine. It also goes farther and faster than an electric car. Hybrids go farther on a gallon of gas for several reasons. They have smaller, lighter engines. Also, the engine of a hybrid car is not always running. When a driver waits for a light to change to green or sits in traffic, the engine shuts off.

The batteries keep the radio playing and the lights on. Then, when the car starts moving again, the engine comes back on.

3. What structure is used in this paragraph? How do you know?
   Description Because thay are Disribing the car and how it works

Writers may use more than one kind of text structure in an article. They may compare in one paragraph and use cause and effect in another. As you read, pay attention to clues that the text structure is changing.

Will Cities Make the Switch?

Some cities think hybrid cars are a good idea. New York City is famous for its many taxi cabs. All these cabs cause air pollution. The city has plans to replace all the gas cabs with hybrid cabs by the year 2012. One thousand hybrid cabs will be in use by 2008. The hybrid cabs cost more. However, drivers will save about $10,000 per year in gas bills.

4. What new structure is used in this paragraph?
   Comper and contros

When you know an article's text structure, you can summarize the important ideas of each part of the structure. To summarize, retell the important ideas in your own words. Use the same text structure in your summary. This will help you remember the most important information in the article you just read.

Not every city is pleased with hybrid cars. Philadelphia, for example, bought 20 hybrid cars. However, city officials think that the extra cost of these cars is not paying off. They may have to wait a few years. After hybrids have been around for longer, they may cost less.

5. Write a summary of this paragraph. Use the same text structure you see in the paragraph.
   hybrid cars are great for the inviroment but thay are very expese.

6. Now write a summary of the whole article using the text structures you identified.
   hybrid cars run on Battery and gas to keep the vorlD cleaner But, thay can Be very exper.

7. How else can you use summarizing to help you understand text structure?

8. What questions do you have about why you should identify a text's structure?

Unit 5   3

Learn the Skill

Quick Recall of Basic Multiplication Facts

Learn the SKILL

Sarit wants to know how many vases she can put 24 flowers in, if she puts the same number of flowers in each vase. How can Sarit use her knowledge of basic multiplication facts to quickly find the number of vases she could use?

SKILL	EXAMPLE	WRITE AN EXAMPLE
Factors are numbers that are multiplied together to give a certain product. Knowing the factors of different numbers can help you multiply more quickly. The factors of different numbers can be found in pairs. To find all the factors of a number, first list 1 and the number. Then check 2, 3, 4, and so on. Write each pair of factors. When the factors in your list start to repeat, you can quickly find the rest of the factor pairs by reversing the order of factors you have already written. You can do this because of the commutative property of multiplication.	How many different ways can you put 24 objects into equal groups? Use pairs of factors to find multiplication facts for 24 until the factors start to repeat: $1 \times 24, 2 \times 12, 3 \times 8, 4 \times 6, 6 \times 4$ The factors 4 and 6 are repeated. To find the rest of the factors, reverse the order of factors you already found: $8 \times 3, 12 \times 2, 24 \times 1$ The eight factors of 24 are 1, 2, 3, 4, 6, 8, 12, and 24. These are the possible numbers of groups you can use.	Write a number between 10 and 30. *20* Write the multiplication facts for your number. *10X2=20 4X5=20* *1X20=20* How many factors does the number have? *6* What are the possible numbers of groups you can use to evenly divide your number? *10, 2, 4, 5, 1, 20*
What is another way to find factor pairs? After you find one multiplication fact for a number, you can use it to find other facts. For example, you can try doubling the first factor and dividing the second factor by 2.	What are some factor pairs for 36? The number 36 is even, so 2 is a factor. Use these two facts: $2 \times 18 = 36$; two groups of 18 is 36 $18 \times 2 = 36$; 18 groups of 2 is 36 You can double 2 and divide 18 by 2 to find two more multiplication facts for 36: $4 \times 9 = 36$ $9 \times 4 = 36$	Write an even multiple of 4 that is greater than 10. *8* Write a multiplication fact for the number. *4X2=8* Use the multiplication fact to find another multiplication fact. *2X4=8*

YOUR TURN

Choose the Right Word

> commutative property   factors   multiply

Fill in each blank with the correct word or phrase from the box.

1. The _factors_ of a number are two numbers that are multiplied together to get that number.

2. The _commutaive propety_ of multiplication can help you find all the factor pairs of a number.

3. One way to _multiply_ more quickly is to learn the factors of different numbers.

Yes or No?

Answer these questions and be ready to explain your answers.

4. Is 1 a factor of all numbers? _yes_

5. Does 25 have three different factors? _yes_

6. Do any numbers have only two factors? _yes_

7. Does zero have any factors? _yes_

Show That You Know

Write the pairs of factors for each number.

8. 15   3, 5

9. 12   6, 2

10. 23   1, 23

11. 25   5, 5

12. 32   4, 8

Find all the factors and list them from least to greatest.

13. factors of 45: 1, 5, 9, 45

14. factors of 49: 1, 7, 49

15. factors of 60: 1, 2, 5, 6, 10, 12, 30, 60

16. factors of 100: 1, 2, 5, 10, 20, 50, 100

Unit 5, Lesson 1

Learn the Skill

SOLVE on Your Own

Skills Practice

List all the factor pairs for each number.

Do not forget to use 1 and the number itself as a factor pair.

1. 11 1, 11,

2. 28 1, 28, 2, 14, 7, 4

3. 35 1, 35, 5, 7

4. 36 1, 36, 12, 3, 9, 4, 6, 2

5. 42 1, 42, 2, 21, 7, 6

6. 75 1, 75,

7. 81 1, 81, 9, 2

List all the factors for each number from least to greatest.

8. 17 1, 17

9. 33 1, 3, 11, 33

10. 63 1, 7, 9, 63

11. 54 1, 6, 9, 54, 5

12. 56 1, 7, 8, 56

13. 66 1, 2, 6, 11, 33, 66

14. 72 1, 6, 8, 9, 12, 72

15. 80 1, 2, 8, 10, 40, 80

How many different factors does each number have? Write your answer on the line.

16. 9 3   19. 39 2

17. 27 4   20. 42 6

18. 29 2

Unit 5, Lesson 1

Choose a Strategy

Quick Recall of Basic Multiplication Facts

Strategies

Draw a Picture or Use a Model, Make a List

Step 1: Read You and your friends are trying to divide up free movie tickets for a raffle fund drive. You have 16 tickets. Each winner must receive the same number of raffle tickets. You want the number of movie tickets each winner receives to be greater than the total number of winners. For example, you cannot have eight winners each receive two movie tickets each. What are some possible combinations of winners and numbers of tickets?

STRATEGY	SOLUTION
Draw a Picture or Use a Model (area model) Area models can be used to show factors of a number. Use the factors to find pairs of factors that satisfy the conditions in the problem.	**Step 2: Plan** Find area models of 16 boxes with more columns than rows. These models represent groups of tickets that are greater than the number of winners. **Step 3: Solve** Area models representing 16 boxes that satisfy these conditions include 1×16 and 2×8. The raffle can have 1 or 2 winners. The winners will receive 16 or 8 movie tickets. **Step 4: Check** Use multiplication to make sure the total number of tickets is 16. $1 \times 16 = 16$ $2 \times 8 = 16$
Make a List You can make a list of the factor pairs of a number. Write down all possible combinations of factors. Once you have listed all the possible pairs, you can test each pair to see whether they satisfy the conditions of the problem.	**Step 2: Plan** Make a list of factor pairs of 16. In this list, have the first number represent the number of winners. Have the second number represent the number of movie tickets. **Step 3: Solve** Factor pairs for 16: 1. 1, 16 2. 2, 8 3. 4, 4 4. 8, 2 5. 16, 1 The only pairs in which the first factor is smaller than the second are the first two pairs. These are the possible combinations of numbers of winners and tickets given to each winner. **Step 4: Check** Use division to check whether the factor pairs are correct. $16 \div 1 = 16$ $16 \div 2 = 8$

Unit 5, Lesson 2

Choose a Strategy

YOUR TURN

Choose the Right Word

area model   factor   make a list

Fill in each blank with the correct word or phrase from the box.

1. When you __make a list__, you write down all possible combinations.

2. A(n) __area model__ can be used to find the factors of a number.

3. Every number has at least one __factor__ pair that can be multiplied together to make the number.

Yes or No?

Answer these questions and be ready to explain your answers.

4. Is it possible for a number to be represented by only one area model? __yes__

5. Does any number have only one factor pair? __no__

6. Is an area model representing 3 × 4 different than an area model representing 4 × 3? __no__

7. Does an area model representing 3 × 4 represent a different number than an area model representing 4 × 3? __no__

Show That You Know

Draw area models to find the factor pairs of the number below.

8. 12
1, 12
2, 6
3, 4

List all the factor pairs of the numbers below.

9. 16   1, 16, 2, 8, 4, 4

10. 33   1, 33, 11, 3

11. 59   1, 59

Unit 5, Lesson 2

READ on Your Own

Reading Comprehension Strategy: Text Structure

Transportation: Past to Future, *pages 3–4*

Before You Read

Think about the different ways that you get from one place to another. How might these be different from the ways your great-grandparents got from place to place?

As You Read

Preview and read "Getting from Here to There," pages 3–4. Fill in the chart below.

What I Learned from the First Paragraph	What I Learned from the Last Paragraph	What I Learned About How the Article Begins and Ends
_____	_____	_____
_____	_____	_____
_____	_____	_____
_____	_____	_____
_____	_____	_____
_____	_____	_____

After You Read

What modern forms of transportation might you use to go exploring today?

_____

_____

VOCABULARY

Watch for the words you are learning about.

corps: a group that acts toward a common goal

species: a group of plants, animals, or insects that share many common characteristics

transportation: a means for carrying people, animals, or things from one place to another

Fluency Tip

To help you read with expression, pretend you are reading aloud to a friend.

Problem Solving

SOLVE on Your Own

Transportation: Past to Future, *page 5*

Organize the Information

Read You Do the Math in the magazine. Then fill out the following table with possible planned hikes. One hike has been filled in for you.

Listing multiples of both 4 and 8 may help you solve the magazine problem.

Planned Hikes

Hike	Easy Days (4 mi)	Easy Miles	Advanced Days (8 mi)	Advanced Miles	Total Miles
32-mile hike	4	16	2	16	32
40-mile hike					
56-mile hike					
65-mile hike					

You Do the Math

Use the information in the table above to answer these questions. Write your answers in the space provided.

1. A tour group wants to do a 65-mile hike. Is it possible to come up with a number of easy and advanced days that gives you an exact total of 65 miles?

   _____
   _____

2. What patterns do you see in the multiples of 4 and 8 that could help you solve this problem?

   _____
   _____

After You Solve

You learned about the trails Lewis and Clark traveled. Do you think it would be easier or harder for you to hike the same trails? Explain.

_____
_____

10   Unit 5, Lesson 2

Quick Recall of Basic Division Facts

Learn the SKILL

VOCABULARY
Watch for the words you are learning about.

divisible: able to be divided evenly by another number

Albert wants to arrange 360 boxes of cereal in a display at the grocery store. He wants to arrange the boxes in groups of 2, 3, 4, 5, 6, 8, 9, or 10. What is the fastest way for him to determine if 360 is divisible by each of these numbers?

SKILL	EXAMPLE	WRITE AN EXAMPLE
A number is **divisible** by another number when their quotient is a whole number. Simple tests can help you tell whether a number is divisible by another number. Divisible by 2: The last digit is 0, 2, 4, 6, or 8. Divisible by 4: The last two digits form a number divisible by 4. Divisible by 8: The last three digits form a number divisible by 8.	Is 360 divisible by 2? Yes, it ends with 0, an even number. Is 360 divisible by 4? Yes, it ends with 60 and 60 is divisible by 4. Is 25,360 divisible by 8? Yes, it ends with 360 and 360 is divisible by 8.	Write a three-digit number divisible by 2: _____ How do you know your number is divisible by 2? _____ Write a four-digit number divisible by 4 but not by 8: _____ How do you know your number is correct? _____ _____
Divisible by 3: The sum of the digits is divisible by 3. Divisible by 6: The rules for both 2 and 3 apply. Divisible by 9: The sum of the digits is divisible by 9.	Is 360 divisible by 3? Yes, 3 + 6 + 0 = 9, and 9 is divisible by 3. Is 360 divisible by 6? Yes, since 360 ends in 0 and is divisible by 3. Is 360 divisible by 9? Yes, 3 + 6 + 0 = 9, and 9 is divisible by 9.	Write a three-digit number divisible by 3 but not by 9: _____ How do you know your number is correct? _____ Write a three-digit number divisible by 6: _____ How do you know your number is divisible by 6? _____
Divisible by 5: The last digit is 5 or 0. Divisible by 10: The last digit is 0.	Is 360 divisible by 5? Yes, it ends with 0. Is 360 divisible by 10? Yes, it ends with 0.	Write a three-digit number divisible by 5 but not 10: _____ How do you know your number is correct? _____

Unit 5, Lesson 3

Learn the Skill

YOUR TURN

Choose the Right Word

divisible   product   quotient

Fill in each blank with the correct word or phrase from the box.

1. The _____ is the answer to a division problem.

2. A number is _____ by another number when their quotient is a whole number.

3. The _____ is the answer to a multiplication problem.

Yes or No?

Answer these questions and be ready to explain your answers.

4. If a number is divisible by 6 is it divisible by 3? _____

5. Can a number be divisible by 10 and not by 5? _____

6. If a number is divisible by 2 must it be divisible by 8? _____

7. Is it possible to divide 125 by 3 evenly? _____

Show That You Know

Use the tests to find out if each number is divisible by 2, 3, or 5.

8. 248 is divisible by

9. 195 is divisible by

10. 771 is divisible by

11. 7,620 is divisible by

12. 8,813 is divisible by

Use the tests to find out if each number is divisible by 4, 9, or 10.

13. 724 is divisible by

14. 810 is divisible by

15. 2,322 is divisible by

16. 5,120 is divisible by

12   Unit 5, Lesson 3

SOLVE on Your Own

Skills Practice

The tests can also help you find the factors of a number.

Write if the following numbers are divisible by 2, 3, 4, 5, 6, 8, 9, or 10. Write "none" if the number is divisible by none of these numbers.

1. 258 is divisible by _____

2. 495 is divisible by _____

3. 371 is divisible by _____

4. 240 is divisible by _____

5. 987 is divisible by _____

6. 844 is divisible by _____

7. 772 is divisible by _____

8. 1,158 is divisible by _____

9. 2,875 is divisible by _____

10. 5,542 is divisible by _____

11. 6,843 is divisible by _____

12. 4,284 is divisible by _____

13. 9,810 is divisible by _____

14. 3,366 is divisible by _____

15. 68,412 is divisible by _____

16. 41,238 is divisible by _____

17. 22,107 is divisible by _____

18. 33,160 is divisible by _____

19. 11,111 is divisible by _____

20. 36,000 is divisible by _____

Choose a Strategy

Quick Recall of Basic Division Facts

Strategies

**Try a Simpler Form of the Problem;
Guess, Check, and Revise**

Step 1: Read Juan recently went on a family vacation to Washington, D.C. During the flight, the captain of the airplane announced that she was flying at an elevation of 32,000 feet. How could you find about how many miles 32,000 feet would be? Remember that 1 mile is equal to 5,280 feet, or about 5,000 feet.

STRATEGY	SOLUTION
Try a Simpler Form of the Problem Rounding the numbers used in a problem can allow you to use numbers that are easier to work with. Since an exact answer is not necessary, it is fine to use compatible numbers rather than the numbers you are given.	**Step 2: Plan** Find compatible numbers and round the amounts to two numbers that are easily divisible. Divide to find the number of miles. **Step 3: Solve** 30 and 5 are compatible numbers. Round 32,000 down to the nearest ten thousand and use 5,000 for 5,280 feet. Divide: 30,000 ÷ 5,000 = 30 ÷ 5 = 6 miles **Step 4: Check** Multiply to check: 6 × 5,000 = 30,000.
Guess, Check, and Revise A first estimate should be obtained by using the numbers of the problem to make an educated guess. Using an educated first guess can help reduce the number of revisions needed to close in on the answer.	**Step 2: Plan** Guess an initial answer by comparing 32,000 feet to about 5,280 feet. Check the guess using multiplication. **Step 3: Solve** Guess: 5 miles Check: 5,280 feet × 5 = 26,400 feet 32,000 feet − 26,400 feet = 5,600 feet, which is greater than one mile. Revise: The initial guess is too low. Increase the guess by one mile. Guess: 6 miles Check: 5,280 feet × 6 = 31,680 feet 32,000 − 31,680 = 320 feet. Six miles is a good estimate of your elevation. **Step 4: Check** Round both numbers down and divide to check: 30,000 ÷ 5,000 = 6.

YOUR TURN

Choose the Right Word

> compatible numbers   dividend   divisor

Fill in each blank with the correct word or phrase from the box.

1. When you use _____, you estimate an answer using numbers that are easier to divide.

2. In division you divide by the _____.

3. In division the number that is divided is the _____.

Choose a Strategy

Yes or No?

Answer these questions and be ready to explain your answers.

4. Does the first guess of an answer affect the Revise step? _____

5. Is it possible to use the Guess, Check, and Revise strategy without revising? _____

6. Are compatible numbers always higher than the original numbers? _____

7. When estimating in division, do you always round the numbers up? _____

Show That You Know

Change one or both numbers to compatible numbers and divide.

8. 88 ÷ 9
   ___ ÷ ___ = ___

9. 216 ÷ 8
   ___ ÷ ___ = ___

10. 57 ÷ 3
    ___ ÷ ___ = ___

11. 163 ÷ 8
    ___ ÷ ___ = ___

Guess, check, and revise answers to each division problem. Show your work.

12. 500 ÷ 125 =

    Guess:

    Check:

    Revise:

13. 1,200 ÷ 240 =

    Guess:

    Check:

    Revise:

Unit 5, Lesson 4

Reading Comprehension

READ on Your Own

Reading Comprehension Strategy: Text Structure

Transportation: Past to Future, pages 6–7

VOCABULARY

Watch for the words you are learning about.

caravans: groups of vehicles that travel together

transcontinental: crossing an entire continent

Fluency Tip

Skim the passage for words that are hard to pronounce. Practice reading these words ahead of time.

Before You Read

Think about what you read in "Getting from Here to There." What methods of transportation do you think early Americans used to move West?

As You Read

Read "The Golden Spike," pages 6–7. 🛑

In the chart below, describe three problems faced by the railroad companies in building a transcontinental railroad. Then describe how each problem was solved. The first one has been done for you.

The Problems	The Solutions
1. There was no money for the railroad.	1. Congress passed the Pacific Railroad Act.
2. _____	2. _____
3. _____	3. _____

After You Read

What problems might railroad companies face if they attempted to build a new railroad across the country today?

_____

_____

16   Unit 5, Lesson 4

Problem Solving

SOLVE on Your Own

Transportation: Past to Future, page 8

Organize the Information

Read You Do the Math in the magazine. Then complete the following table with information on the work crews and the time needed to complete each section of track.

Miles	Compatible Miles	Number of Work Crews	Total Miles per Week	Total Weeks
211	212	1		
		2		
		3		
42	44	1		
		2		
		3		
409	408	1		
		2		
		3		
24	24	1		
		2		
		3		

Listing multiples of the total miles per week may help you answer the magazine questions.

You Do the Math

Use the information in the table to answer these questions. Write your answers in the space provided.

1. How can finding compatible numbers of miles help you estimate the number of weeks?

_____

2. If you only had 26 weeks to get the most track laid, where would you send your crews? Explain.

_____

_____

After You Solve

What things do you think modern trains are used for?

_____

Unit 5, Lesson 4   17

Application

Solve It!

The Four-Step Problem-Solving Plan

Step 1: Read	Step 2: Plan	Step 3: Solve	Step 4: Check
Make sure you understand what the problem is asking.	Decide how you will solve the problem.	Solve the problem using your plan.	Check to make sure your answer is correct.

Read the article below. Then answer the questions.

Not Just Gasoline-Powered

One of the major problems with cars is the amount of pollution they produce. As a result, some car companies have begun producing cars that do not pollute as much as gasoline-powered cars. One example is the electric car. More companies are designing better electric cars as a choice for customers who care about the environment.

This is not the first time that electric cars have been used in America. At the beginning of the 20th century, many Americans used electricity to power their cars. However, the environment was not the reason. People liked these cars because they were easier to use than gasoline-powered cars. The driver did not have to wait for water to heat in order to start the car on a cold day. Also, people did not have to get out of their cars to start them, which they had to do with early gasoline-powered cars.

1. One of Henry Ford's gasoline-powered cars was sold for $500 in the same year that an electric car sold for $3,000. For what fraction of the price of the electric car did the gasoline-powered car sell?

   _____

2. In 1899 an electric racing car, *La Jamais Contente*, set a world record for a top land speed of 68 mph. In 1902 an electric car called Phaeton had a top land speed of 14 mph. About how many times faster was the racing car than the Phaeton? Round your answer.

   _____

YOUR TURN

Application

Read the article below. Then answer the questions.

Rise of the Gasoline-Powered Car

Even though electric cars were admired, there were several reasons they were not as popular. For example, it took a long time to charge the battery. Also, they did not travel as quickly as other types of cars.

Buyers turned their attention to the gasoline-powered cars. Improvements made in the production of the gasoline-powered car meant that drivers no longer had to get out of the car to start it. Drivers also expected more from their cars. They liked being able to drive longer distances without recharging them. At first this was considered a luxury, but soon it became a "must-have."

Henry Ford also had a lot to do with the success of gasoline-powered cars. As vice president of the Ford Motor Company, Henry Ford was the first to build cars on an assembly line. This way of making cars led to cheaper prices. By 1927, 15 million of the Model T Ford cars were on the road.

Fluency Tip
Pay attention to punctuation marks. Punctuation marks tell you when to pause and when to raise your voice for a question or an exclamation.

1. In 1927, there were about 119 million people living in the United States. If there were 15 million Model T cars on the road, about how many people were there for each car?

_____
_____

2. How did the popularity of the gasoline-powered car change?

_____
_____
_____

3. In 1914, Henry Ford paid his workers $5 a day. If he budgeted $5,000 for each five-day work week, how many employees would he be able to pay?

_____
_____

Unit 5, Lesson 5

Reading Comprehension

READ on Your Own

Reading Comprehension Strategy: Text Structure

Transportation: Past to Future, pages 9–11

Before You Read

Think about the journeys of the early Americans you read about in "The Golden Spike." How did the types of transportation improve over the years?

As You Read

Read "Cars Then and Now," pages 9–11. 🛑

Read the two statements about cars in the chart below. Write whether they are comparing or contrasting two things.

Statement	Comparison or Contrast?	How Do You Know?
In the 1930s, cars were produced with a wheelbase of up to 13 feet. Cars with a smaller wheelbase, closer to 8 feet...took up less space.		
Some people thought that Cugnot's steam-powered car looked like an overgrown tricycle.		

After You Read

What is the most interesting thing you have learned about the history of cars?

_____

_____

_____

VOCABULARY

Watch for the words you are learning about.

hybrid: something that has two parts that can do the same thing

wheelbase: the distance between front and back wheels

Fluency Tip

As you read and reread, pay attention to punctuation marks that are clues to correct phrasing.

Problem Solving

SOLVE on Your Own

Transportation: Past to Future, page 12

Organize the Information

Read the Math Project in the magazine. Then fill out the table below to decide which types of cars you should sell.

Touring ($600 each)	Runabout ($525 each)	Town Car ($800 each)	Delivery Car ($625 each)	Total Sales	Total Assembly Lines Needed
75	0	0	24	$60,000	4

Math Project

Use the information in the table above to answer these questions. Write your answers in the space provided.

> If you guess the numbers of each car to make, check your answers and revise if needed.

1. Is it possible to make all the cars you need to sell using only three assembly lines? Explain your answer.

   _____
   _____

2. Which cars and how many of each car must you choose to make in order to reach your sales target? Explain your answer.

   _____
   _____

After You Solve

Does it make more sense to make more of the Runabout (the cheapest car) or the Touring Car (the most expensive)?

_____
_____
_____

Unit 5, Lesson 5

Learn the Skill

Multiplying Multidigit Numbers Using Models

Learn the SKILL

> **VOCABULARY**
> Watch for the words you are learning about.
>
> **interval:** the space or time between things
>
> **multidigit number:** a number with more than one digit

Ms. Graham has 12 students in her class. Each student brings 13 pennies for a class project. How many pennies will the class have in total?

SKILL	EXAMPLE	COMPLETE THE EXAMPLE
Multiplication can be represented using an array. The first factor is the number of rows and the second factor is the number of columns. The product is the total number of objects. To simplify finding the number of objects, circle groups of 100, and then groups of 10. Count the ones remaining and add all three groups. This method is useful when multiplying **multidigit numbers.**	Create an array to show 12 × 13 as dots.	Create an array to show 11 × 11.
Multiplication also can be represented using an area model, which is shown as boxes grouped in a rectangle. The first factor is the number of rows and the second factor is the number of columns. To simplify finding the number of boxes, color groups of 100 one color and each group of 10 another color. Then count the ones remaining and add all three groups.	Create an area model of 12 × 13.	Create an area model of 11 × 11.
A number line can also show multiplication by skip-counting using the second factor as the **interval,** or size of the jump. The first factor gives the total number of jumps.	Show 12 × 13 as jumping by 13 twelve times. The second factor, 13, is the interval.	Show 11 × 11 as intervals on a number line.

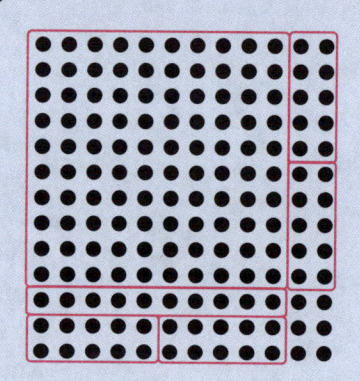

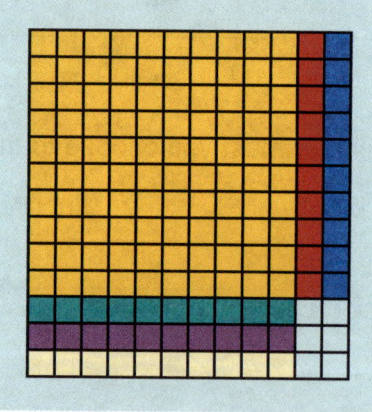

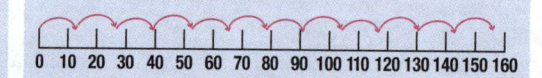

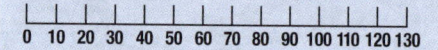

Unit 5, Lesson 6

YOUR TURN

Choose the Right Word

> area model   array   interval
> multidigit number

Fill in each blank with the correct word or phrase from the box.

1. A(n) _____ is an arrangement of objects in rows and columns.

2. A(n) _____ is an arrangement of boxes in a rectangle.

3. A _____ is a number that is more than one digit.

4. The size of the jumps on a number line is their _____.

Yes or No?

Answer these questions and be ready to explain your answers.

5. Does an array use pictures? _____

6. Is 7 a multidigit number? _____

7. Is 77 a multidigit number? _____

8. To represent 8 × 15 on a number line, can you make eight jumps at intervals of 15? _____

Learn the Skill

Show That You Know

Write the number of rows and columns you would use to draw an array or area model.

9. 15 × 25

10. 17 × 12

11. 13 × 16

12. 11 × 10

13. 12 × 14

Write the intervals and the number of jumps you would use to solve these problems with a number line.

14. 12 × 25   Interval:
    Jumps:

15. 11 × 15   Interval:
    Jumps:

16. 16 × 10   Interval:
    Jumps:

17. 11 × 20   Interval:
    Jumps:

Unit 5, Lesson 6

Learn the Skill

SOLVE on Your Own

Skills Practice

> Remember, you skip-count by the second factor. The number of jumps is given by the first factor.

Multiply. Check your answer using addition.

How many rows and columns would you make in an array or area model?

1. 10 × 16 _____
2. 4 × 12 _____
3. 8 × 11 _____

On a sheet of paper, draw an array or area model for the expressions in 1–3. Write the product on the line.

4. 10 × 16 = _____
5. 4 × 12 = _____
6. 8 × 11 = _____

Write the intervals and the number of jumps you would use to show the amount on a number line. Then draw a number line or skip count to multiply.

7. 18 × 20 = _____

   Interval: _____

   Jumps: _____

8. 20 × 8 = _____

   Interval: _____

   Jumps: _____

24 Unit 5, Lesson 6

Multiplying Multidigit Numbers Using Models

Strategies
Draw a Picture or Use a Model,
Try a Simpler Form of the Problem

Choose a Strategy

VOCABULARY
Watch for the words you are learning about.

overestimate: to round up; to guess more than you think your answer will be

underestimate: to round down; to guess less than you think your answer will be

Step 1: Read Last year Nikki attended summer school for 19 days. Each morning before school she waited about 8 minutes for the bus. What was the total time she spent waiting for the bus?

STRATEGY	SOLUTION
Draw a Picture or Use a Model Many problems can be solved by estimating a solution. When there is not enough information to give an exact answer to a problem, you can **overestimate** or **underestimate** to find the range of possible answers. After you estimate, you can model the problem with an array to find the product.	**Step 2: Plan** Find the least amount of time Nikki could have spent waiting for the bus. Then find the greatest amount of time she could have spent waiting for the bus. The actual time spent waiting will be between these values. **Step 3: Solve** Least waiting time: round 8 down to 5. 19 days × $\frac{5 \text{ minutes}}{\text{day}}$ Draw a 19 × 5 array. 19 × 5 = 95 minutes Greatest waiting time: round 8 up to 10. 19 days × $\frac{10 \text{ minutes}}{\text{day}}$ Draw a 19 × 10 array. 19 × 10 = 190 minutes The actual waiting time was between 95 and 190 minutes. **Step 4: Check** Draw a number line from 0 to 200 and skip-count by 5 nineteen times to find 19 × 5. Then skip-count by 10 nineteen times to find 19 × 10.
Try a Simpler Form of the Problem An estimate does not need to be exact. Use numbers that are easier to work with to find a number that is close to the exact answer.	**Step 2: Plan** Round 19 days to an easier number and multiply it by 8 to estimate the total waiting time. **Step 3: Solve** Round 19 to 20. Draw an area model that represents 20 × 8 and count the squares. 20 days × $\frac{8 \text{ minutes}}{\text{day}}$ = 160 minutes **Step 4: Check** Divide your area model into equal groups to check your multiplication: 160 ÷ 8 = 20.

Choose a Strategy

YOUR TURN

Choose the Right Word

estimate   overestimate   underestimate

Fill in each blank with the correct word or phrase from the box.

1. When you _____, you find a number that is larger than the true answer.

2. To _____, round one or more of the factors down.

3. When an exact answer cannot be found, a(n) _____ can be made instead.

Yes or No?

Answer these questions and be ready to explain your answers.

4. Can an estimate ever be equal to the true answer of a problem? _____

5. Can rounding be used to estimate an answer to a problem? _____

6. When an estimate is made, do the values used in multiplication change the accuracy of the estimate? _____

7. Is a true answer ever less than an underestimate? _____

Show That You Know

Round one or both of the numbers up to overestimate the answer.

8. 24 × 9

   ____ × ____ = ____

9. 19 × 55

   ____ × ____ = ____

10. 39 × 20

    ____ × ____ = ____

Round one or both of the numbers down to underestimate the exact answer.

11. 250 × 12

    ____ × ____ = ____

12. 142 × 10

    ____ × ____ = ____

13. 32 × 33

    ____ × ____ = ____

Unit 5, Lesson 7

Reading Comprehension

READ on Your Own

Reading Comprehension Strategy: Text Structure

Transportation: Past to Future, pages 13–14

VOCABULARY

Watch for the words you are learning about.

average speed: the typical speed at which an object is traveling, calculated by dividing the distance traveled by the time taken to travel that distance

voyage: journey, often by water or air

Fluency Tip

Remember to read smoothly. Try to read phrases instead of individual words.

Before You Read

Think about what you read in "Cars Then and Now." What type of car might you have driven if you lived in the early 1900s or in the 1950s?

As You Read

Read "Another Kind of Air Travel," pages 13–14. 🛑
Fill in the chart below with information about the facts and opinions in what you have read.

Find This	What I Found
an opinion by the author in the first paragraph on page 13	
a fact about the Montgolfier hot air balloon	
an opinion by the author in the last paragraph on page 14	
a fact about the record for the highest flying hot air balloon	

After You Read

You are the captain of a hot air balloon. What would you do to make your balloon go faster?

Unit 5, Lesson 7

Problem Solving

SOLVE on Your Own

Transportation: Past to Future, page 15

Organize the Information

Read You Do the Math in the magazine. Then fill out the following table with information on the speed, flight times, and distances traveled by the blimp.

Speed of blimp: 35 mph
Speed of blimp (rounded):

Time of Flight (hours)	Estimated Distance (miles)	Exact Distance (miles)
3		
6		
10		

Drawing a map or another picture to show distances between cities may help you answer the magazine questions.

You Do the Math

Use the information in the table above to answer these questions. Write your answers in the space provided.

1. Could you eliminate any of the options before doing any calculations? Explain.

2. If you round the miles per hour up to 40, what can you assume about your estimated product?

3. Which cities would you choose as destinations for each length of trip? Explain your reasoning.

After You Solve

Why do you think people want to travel using faster modes of transportation? Can you think of a reason why someone might still want to travel by blimp?

Unit 5, Lesson 7

Solve It!

Application

The Four-Step Problem-Solving Plan

Step 1: Read	Step 2: Plan	Step 3: Solve	Step 4: Check
Make sure you understand what the problem is asking.	Decide how you will solve the problem.	Solve the problem using your plan.	Check to make sure your answer is correct.

Read the article below. Then answer the questions.

Under the City

Originally, there were three privately-owned subway companies in New York City. The Brooklyn Union Elevated Railroad Company was the first to build tracks that ran above ground from Brooklyn to Manhattan. When it joined the other independently-owned Brooklyn train companies, it became known as the Brooklyn Rapid Transit Corporation. The name was later changed to the Brooklyn, Manhattan Transit Corporation (BMT). You can still ride the BMT line today.

The Manhattan-based Interborough Rapid Transit (IRT) controlled all of the trains that ran through Manhattan, the Bronx, and Brooklyn. When the city made plans to join some of the tracks of the BMT and IRT, both companies agreed to share some track lines.

A third subway system, The Independent Subway (IND), was created to help reduce over-crowding. The IRT was built to hold a maximum of 600,000 daily passengers. Instead, it was carrying a daily load of 800,000 passengers. A few years later this number increased to 1.2 million. A plan was needed to make the system bigger and more connected.

1. Describe the origins of the New York City subway.

   _____
   _____
   _____

2. Suppose the IND had 50 subway cars and the BMT had half as many subway cars. If the IRT had twice as many subway cars as IND and BMT combined, how many cars would the IRT have?

   _____

Unit 5, Lesson 8

Application

YOUR TURN

Read the article below. Then answer the questions.

Not-So-Smooth Merger

The subway in New York City is famous throughout the world. Every day, millions of people ride a single subway service throughout four regions of the city. At the beginning of the century, however, a rider would have been unable to ride the same subway from the Bronx through Manhattan and into Brooklyn.

To make it easier to travel across the city, the government took over the three different subway lines and tried to join them. However, there were big problems. Each company had trains and stations built to different measurements. Also, the city had to build lines into areas that had no service, and cut back service from areas that had too much. The city also had to set up free transfer points between stations. This way, passengers could move from one line to another without paying another fare. The process of joining the lines was long and difficult, but eventually it worked.

Fluency Tip
Change your expression as you read.

1. Imagine the city set up one free transfer point between every three stations on a line. If there were 129 stations in all, how many transfer points were set up?

   _____

2. What issues came up when the city tried to merge the three subway lines?

   _____
   _____
   _____
   _____

3. How do you think joining the three subway lines have made the system better?

   _____
   _____
   _____
   _____

READ on Your Own

Reading Comprehension Strategy: Text Structure

Transportation: Past to Future, pages 16–18

Before You Read

Consider the hot air balloons you read about in "Another Form of Air Travel." How does a hot air balloon work?

As You Read

Read "New York's Secret Subway," pages 16–18.
Then complete the chart below.

VOCABULARY

Watch for the words you are learning about.

experiment: a test used to decide whether a hypothesis could be true

hypothesis: an idea that can be tested by experiment

pneumatic tubes: narrow pipes that use blasts of air to move objects short distances

Fluency Tip

If you find yourself reading so quickly that you are missing the meaning, slow down.

What I Learned About the First Subways	What I Learned About Alfred Ely Beach	What I Learned About New York's Subway Today

After You Read

How has the subway affected the lives of people in cities with subway systems?

Unit 5, Lesson 8

Problem Solving

SOLVE on Your Own

Transportation: Past to Future, page 19

Organize the Information

Read the Math Project in the magazine. Then use the information to complete the table based on the cost of a single ride and a 7-Day Unlimited Ride Card.

	Jenna	Ali	Steve
Number of trips per week			
Cost if paying per ride			
Cost if using Unlimited Ride Card			

Math Project

Use the information in the table to answer these questions. Write your answers in the space provided.

You can use arrays to represent the number of rides each person takes per week.

1. What makes Ali's information harder to deal with?

   _____
   _____

2. What strategy would you recommend for each rider? Explain your answers.

   _____
   _____
   _____

After You Solve

What other type of graphic organizer could be used to display the information in the table?

_____
_____

32   Unit 5, Lesson 8

Put It Together

Introducing Finding Rules for Sequences of Numbers

You have learned several methods for understanding and representing multiplication. These methods can also be used to describe patterns. A sequence is an ordered list of numbers. Here is one example of a sequence: 1, 2, 4, 8, 16, 32.

If you represented these numbers using an array, each array would be twice as big as the previous one. This sequence is created by multiplying a number by 2 to get the next number. It can also be created by adding each number to itself to get the next one. The next three numbers in this sequence are 64, 128, and 256.

| $32 \times 2 = 32 + 32 = 64$ | $64 \times 2 = 64 + 64 = 128$ | $128 \times 2 = 128 + 128 = 256$ |

Here is another type of sequence: 3, 6, 9, 12, 15, 18.

Each number in this sequence is three more than the preceding number. This sequence pattern can also be explained by multiplication. The next three numbers in this sequence are 21, 24, and 27.

| $3 \times 7 = 21$ | $3 \times 8 = 24$ | $3 \times 9 = 27$ |

There is often more than one correct way to describe the pattern in a sequence.

Practicing Finding Rules for Sequences of Numbers

Describe the rule for each sequence and then give the next three numbers.

1. 5, 10, 15, 20, 25   Rule: _____

   Next three numbers: _____

2. 1, 3, 9, 27   Rule: _____

   Next three numbers: _____

3. 1, 10, 100, 1,000

   Rule: _____

   Next three numbers: _____

4. 2, 4, 6, 8, 10   Rule: _____

   Next three numbers: _____

Connections

Unit 5, Lesson 9

Connections

YOUR TURN

Thinking About Finding Rules for Sequences of Numbers

It is a very important for mathematicians to be able to recognize different kinds of patterns. Some sequences are formed with patterns of shapes. These sequences, called geometric patterns, can often be explained and described with both numbers and shapes. Look closely at the geometric pattern below.

1. How many squares are in each shape? _____

2. How many squares would you expect to find in each of the next three shapes?
   _____

3. How could you use multiplication to describe the numerical pattern in the sequence?
   _____

4. What addition pattern could you use to describe the sequence?
   _____

5. What geometric pattern do you see in the sequence?
   _____

6. Draw the next two shapes in the geometric pattern in the space below.

7. Is it easier to determine the next term with the geometric pattern or the numerical pattern?
   _____
   _____

Tip Drawing models can help you understand numerical patterns as well. They can show in another way how numbers in the pattern change.

Unit 5, Lesson 9

Connections

Show That You Know

Read the information below. Use what you have learned about sequences to decide what rules describe the patterns below. Then answer the questions about those sequences.

> Marcus and Zoë plan to enter the same bicycle race. Each set up a five-day training schedule using a different sequence to get ready for the race. On the first day, they will both ride 2 miles. On the second day, they will both ride 4 miles. On the third day, Marcus will ride farther than Zoë.

Ask yourself: Could one pattern have two possible rules? Could two patterns with different rules start out the same?

1. Describe a sequence that starts: 2, 4.

2. What are the next two numbers in the sequence?

3. Describe a different sequence that starts: 2, 4.

4. What are the next two numbers in this sequence?

Unit 5, Lesson 9   35

Connections

Show That You Know (continued)

5. Which sequence is Marcus using for his training schedule? List the numbers of miles for each of the five days.

6. How many miles would Marcus ride on the sixth day?

7. How many miles does Zoë expect to ride on the fifth day of her schedule?

8. If Zoë continues her schedule, when would she ride 32 miles?

9. Can you give a simple rule Zoë can use to find the distance for each day of her schedule?

Review What You've Learned

10. What have you learned in this Connections lesson about sequences using numbers and shapes?

11. How will this lesson help you when you use the Find a Pattern strategy to solve a problem?

Review and Practice

Skills Review

Factors

In a pair of factors, the first factor is the number of groups and the second factor is number in each group. Factor pairs for 25:

1×25, which means 1 group of 25

5×5, which means 5 groups of 5

25×1, which means 25 groups of 1

Quick recall of basic multiplication facts

Given a basic fact, try doubling one factor and halving the other to find another fact:

$2 \times 6 = 12$ is a fact, so

$4 \times 3 = 12$ is another fact.

You can find a fact by reversing the order of the factors in any fact:

$4 \times 5 = 20$ is a fact, so

$5 \times 4 = 20$ also is a fact.

Divisibility tests for

2: last digit is 0, 2, 4, 6, or 8

3: the sum of the digits is a multiple of 3

4: last two digits are divisible by 4

5: the last digit is 5 or 0

6: apply divisibility test for both 2 and 3

8: last three digits are divisible by 8

9: the sum of the digits is a multiple of 9

10: the last digit is 0

Multiplication: Arrays

When creating larger arrays, you can find the total number of objects in the array by circling groups of 100 and groups of 10. Then count the number of ones and add all three groups.

Multiplication: Area models

When creating larger area models, you can find the total number of boxes by coloring in groups of 100 and groups of 10. Then count the number of single boxes and add all three groups.

Multiplication: Number lines

Number lines can be used to skip-count multiples of larger numbers. One example is 32×10. The second factor gives the size of the jumps (the interval, 10), while the first factor gives the total jumps (32).

Strategy Review

- Area models, arrays, and number lines can be used to represent multiplication of both single-digit and multidigit numbers.
- Make an educated guess of the solution, and then check and revise this guess.
- When there is not enough information to find an exact answer, estimate an answer that is between an underestimate and an overestimate.

Unit 5, Lesson 10

Review and Practice

Skills and Strategies Practice

Complete the exercises below.

1. Test 6,210 for divisibility by 2, 3, 4, 5, 6, 8, 9, and 10.
   _____

2. Write the different ways you could put 32 pencils into equal groups:
   _____
   _____
   _____
   _____
   _____

   What are the possible numbers of groups?
   _____

3. Use rounding and compatible numbers to estimate the quotients.

   $79 \div 8$ _____

   $21 \div 4$ _____

   $148 \div 10$ _____

4. Write three factor pairs for 100 that each use different factors.

   _____ × _____ = 100

   _____ × _____ = 100

   _____ × _____ = 100

5. Draw an array to show 5×12.

   What is the product? _____

TEST-TAKING tip

When you start to take a test, quickly look over the entire test. Then decide which questions you will do first and last. For example, for a test on multiplication and division, you may want to do the problems you can finish quickly. Then you can turn to more difficult problems.

Mid-Unit Review

Circle the letter of the correct answer.

1. The number 45 is divisible by _____.

   A. 2 and 5 C. 5 and 9
   B. 5 and 7 D. 2 and 9

2. 12 × 5 = _____

   A. 17 C. 60
   B. 55 D. 65

3. 63 is divisible by _____.

   A. 7 C. 5
   B. 6 D. 4

4. You can estimate 9 × 34 using all the following expressions except _____.

   A. 34 ÷ 9 C. 10 × 34
   B. 9 × 30 D. 10 × 35

5. How many rows and columns would an array for 19 × 22 have?

   A. 19 rows, 19 columns
   B. 22 rows, 22 columns
   C. 19 rows, 22 columns
   D. 22 rows, 19 columns

6. Which answer is a multiplication fact for 36?

   A. 3 × 6 = 36
   B. 9 × 6 = 36
   C. 2 × 18 = 36
   D. 4 × 8 = 36

7. You can estimate 33 ÷ 10 using the expression _____.

   A. 33 ÷ 30
   B. 33 ÷ 1
   C. 30 ÷ 5
   D. 30 ÷ 10

8. 155 is divisible by _____.

   A. 3 C. 8
   B. 5 D. 10

9. 82 is divisible by _____.

   A. 41 C. 12
   B. 20 D. 6

10. An underestimate of 72 ÷ 7 is _____.

    A. 11 C. 12
    B. 10 D. 14

11. 8 × 13 = _____

    A. 8 × 3 × 10
    B. 8 + 10 × 3
    C. 8 × (10 + 3)
    D. 3 × (10 + 8)

12. Estimate the quotient for 124 ÷ 6.

    A. 20 C. 110
    B. 30 D. 118

13. 49 has _____ factors.

    A. 5 C. 3
    B. 4 D. 2

Unit 5, Lesson 10

Review and Practice

Mid-Unit Review

14. 37 is divisible by _____.

A. 2
B. 3
C. 8
D. none of the above

15. The factors of 16 are _____.

A. 2, 3, 8, 16
B. 2, 4, 8, 16
C. 1, 2, 4, 8, 16
D. 0, 1, 2, 4, 8, 16

16. When using a number line to represent 23 × 45, you use an interval of _____ for the jumps.

A. 45
B. 54
C. 23
D. 32

17. How many jumps of an interval of 35 on a number line is 24 × 35?

A. 24
B. 35
C. 840
D. 59

18. 8, 9 is a pair of factors for _____.

A. 63
B. 72
C. 81
D. 90

19. 351 is divisible by _____.

A. 2 and 3
B. 3 and 5
C. 3 and 9
D. 3 and 10

20. 4 × 4 = _____

A. 4 × 8
B. 3 × 8
C. 2 × 8
D. 1 × 8

21. An area model has 34 columns and 24 rows. Which equation does it represent?

A. 24 ÷ 34
B. 34 ÷ 24
C. 34 × 24
D. 24 × 34

22. Which is a pair of factors for 12?

A. 4, 2
B. 4, 4
C. 4, 3
D. 3, 3

23. To multiply 17 × 66, how many jumps might a student make on a number line?

A. 65
B. 17
C. 16
D. 83

24. 16 × 4 is a pair of factors for which number?

A. 4
B. 16
C. 32
D. 64

25. Which is a pair of factors for 15?

A. 4, 3
B. 2, 8
C. 5, 3
D. 3, 3

Multiplying Multidigit Numbers Using the Algorithm

Learn the Skill

VOCABULARY

Watch for the words you are learning about.

partial product: the product of a number and one digit of a multidigit number

regroup: to form into a new grouping; for example, 10 ones become 1 ten and 10 tens become one hundred

Jason picked 85 bushels of apples. He estimates there are 38 apples in each bushel. How many apples has he picked?

SKILL	EXAMPLE	COMPLETE THE EXAMPLE
The most common algorithm for multiplication of multidigit numbers uses a vertical form. Multiply from right to left, starting with the ones. **Regroup** by renaming and carrying any groups of tens. Then multiply the tens and add the **partial products.**	Find the product of 85 × 38. Multiply the ones. Do not forget to add the regrouped tens. 85 × 8 = 680 $$\begin{array}{r} 4 \\ 85 \\ \times\ 38 \\ \hline 680 \end{array}$$ Multiply the tens and then add the partial products. 85 × 30 = 2,550 $$\begin{array}{r} 1 \\ 85 \\ \times\ 38 \\ \hline 680 \\ +\ 2{,}550 \\ \hline 3{,}230 \end{array}$$	Find the product of 14 × 26. Show your work below.
The algorithm can be expanded to calculate products using larger multidigit factors. Multiply each place value in order from left to right.	Find the product of 132 × 176. $$\begin{array}{r} 132 \\ \times\ 176 \\ \hline 792 \\ 9{,}240 \\ +\ 13{,}200 \\ \hline 23{,}232 \end{array}$$ 132 × 6 = 792 132 × 70 = 9,240 132 × 100 = 13,200	Find the product of 176 × 132. Show your work below. Compare your partial products and product to 132 × 176. _____ _____ _____

Unit 5, Lesson 11   41

Learn the Skill

YOUR TURN

Choose the Right Word

> partial product   product   regrouping

Fill in each blank with the correct word or phrase from the box.

1. The _____ is the answer to a multiplication problem.

2. When you carry tens when adding or multiplying, you are _____.

3. The _____ is a number you get by multiplying a number by only one digit of a multidigit number.

Yes or No?

Answer these questions and be ready to explain your answers.

4. When multiplying 15 × 38, is 120 a partial product? _____

5. If 125 is multiplied by 400 are there exactly two zeros in the product? _____

6. Do partial products get added together in the final step of the multiplication algorithm? _____

7. Is the product 43 × 15 the same as the product 15 × 43? _____

Show That You Know

Use the algorithm to find the following products.

8. 15 × 25 =

9. 17 × 39 =

10. 47 × 10 =

11. 756 × 22 =

12. 524 × 18 =

13. 682 × 39 =

14. 267 × 184 =

15. 320 × 110 =

Learn the Skill

SOLVE on Your Own

Skills Practice

Remember to add any regrouped tens, hundreds, or thousands when you multiply multidigit numbers.

Use the algorithm to find the product. Write your answer on the line.

1. 10 × 67 = _____
2. 54 × 39 = _____
3. 86 × 78 = _____
4. 29 × 16 = _____
5. 11 × 92 = _____
6. 136 × 82 = _____
7. 300 × 90 = _____
8. 451 × 25 = _____
9. 387 × 55 = _____
10. 230 × 40 = _____

11. 376 × 39 = _____
12. 785 × 89 = _____
13. 576 × 72 = _____
14. 25 × 379 = _____
15. 32 × 251 = _____
16. 185 × 487 = _____
17. 910 × 195 = _____
18. 232 × 615 = _____
19. 271 × 234 = _____
20. 416 × 668 = _____

Choose a Strategy

Multiplying Multidigit Numbers Using the Algorithm

Strategies

Try a Simpler Form of the Problem, Make a List

Step 1: Read You need to purchase 12 bus tokens for the days that you will be visiting your aunt on the coast. The tokens cost $0.75 each. How can you quickly find the exact cost of 12 tokens?

STRATEGY	SOLUTION
Try a Simpler Form of the Problem Another way to think of the algorithm for multiplying multidigit numbers is to separate the factor into ones, tens, hundreds, and so on, and then use the distributive property multiply. This is similar to the breaking-apart algorithm you have already learned.	**Step 2: Plan** Change the price into cents. Then choose one of the factors to break into a sum of two addends. Multiply each by the other factor and then add. Simplify to find the price in dollars. **Step 3: Solve** Price of one token = $0.75 = 75¢ (cents) Exact cost = 12 × 75¢ Choose a factor: 12 Break the factor apart into a sum: 12 = 2 + 10 Multiply by the other factor: 75¢ × (2 + 10) = 150¢ + 750¢ Add: 150¢ + 750¢ = 900¢ Simplify: 900¢ is equal to 9 dollars ($9) **Step 4: Check** Multiply 12 × 75¢ using vertical form.
Make a List There are many combinations of addends whose sum equals a given number. List the ones you think might be easy to multiply by the second factor.	**Step 2: Plan** List different combinations of addends for both factors. Pair a set of addends with the other factor so that the multiplication is easy to perform. **Step 3: Solve** For 12: 2 + 10; 6 + 6; 8 + 4 For 75¢: 70¢ + 5¢; 40¢ + 35¢; 50¢ + 25¢ Choose a combination: 12 × (70¢ + 5¢) = 840¢ + 60¢ = 900¢, or $9 **Step 4: Check** Divide 900¢ into equal groups of 75¢.

YOUR TURN

Choose the Right Word

> algorithm   combinations
> distributive property

Fill in each blank with the correct word or phrase from the box.

1. Multiplying factors of a number and then adding those sums is allowed by the _____.

2. A(n) _____ is a way of completing a task, such as multiplying two factors.

3. Many different _____ of numbers can add up to a chosen number.

Choose a Strategy

Yes or No?

Answer these questions and be ready to explain your answers.

4. Does the distributive property allow you to find 50 × 36 by multiplying 50 × (30 + 6)? _____

5. Is (30 + 5) × 66 the only way you can rewrite 35 × 66 to make the multiplication easier? _____

6. Is 5 × 4 = 4 × 5 an example of the distributive property of multiplication? _____

7. Is the distributive property required to multiply large numbers? _____

Show That You Know

Split each of the factors to make multiplication easier. List a pair of addends for each factor.

8. 18 × 25

   18 =

   25 =

9. 99 × 31

   99 =

   31 =

Use the distributive property to calculate the following products. Write out the expression you used to find each product.

10. 13 × 21

11. 64 × 44

12. 75 × 16

13. 22 × 22

Unit 5, Lesson 12   45

Reading Comprehension

READ on Your Own

Reading Comprehension Strategy: Text Structure

Transportation: Past to Future, pages 20–21

VOCABULARY

Watch for the words you are learning about.

altitude: the height above Earth's surface

supersonic: traveling faster than the speed of sound

Fluency Tip

Pay attention to punctuation marks. Punctuation marks tell you when to pause and when to raise your voice for a question or an exclamation.

Before You Read

Consider what you learned in "New York's Secret Subway." Would it be practical to build a secret subway in a modern city? Explain.

As You Read

Read "In the Blink of an Eye," pages 20–21. **STOP**

Read the statements below and decide whether they are comparing or contrasting two things.

Statement	Comparison or Contrast?	How Can You Tell?
The Concorde was a supersonic jet that flew faster than the speed of sound.		
Modern trains are much faster than those of the early 1800s.		
The trip from England to France can be completed in only 35 minutes, which is similar to the time it takes to watch a television program.		

After You Read

Why do you think early test pilots referred to going faster than the sound barrier as "breaking" the sound barrier?

46   Unit 5, Lesson 12

Problem Solving

SOLVE on Your Own

Transportation: Past to Future, page 22

Organize the Information

Read You Do the Math in the magazine. Then complete the following table with different possible trips across Europe. The totals should reflect the cost for one person. One plan has been done for you.

Listing all the places you want to go may help you answer the magazine questions.

Plan		Trip 1	Trip 2	Trip 3	Trip 4	Trip 5
1	From Paris	to Prague	to Rome	to Venice	to Paris	
	Total	$226	$476	$548	$725	
2	From Paris					
	Total					
3	From Paris					
	Total					
4	From Paris					
	Total					

You Do the Math

Use the information in the table above to answer these questions. Write your answers in the space provided.

1. Without doing exact calculations, how can you get a general idea of what a trip will cost?
   _____

2. Which itinerary would you recommend? Why?
   _____
   _____

After You Solve

How might the cost of traveling by train compare to the price of using another form of transportation?
_____
_____

Unit 5, Lesson 12   47

Learn the Skill

Mental Calculation

Learn the SKILL

Steve has 38 boxes of thank-you cards. Each box contains 20 cards. He wants to quickly calculate the total number of thank-you cards in his head. What is the best way to estimate how many cards he has? What is the exact count?

SKILL	EXAMPLE	COMPLETE THE EXAMPLE
When attempting to multiply in your head, you should use rounding and estimation to make the problem simpler.	What is a good estimate for the total number of thank-you cards? Round the number of boxes to the nearest 10: 38 becomes 40. A good estimation is $20 \times 40 = 800$.	What is a good estimate of 8×51? _____ How did you round the numbers to find this estimate? _____
If one number ends in 0 it has a factor of 10. Drop the zero, multiply the remaining numbers together, and then multiply by 10. This places a 0 at the end of the number.	Multiply 20×38. First, drop the 0 from 20. Then multiply: $2 \times 38 = 76$. Now multiply by 10: $76 \times 10 = 760$. This means $20 \times 38 = 760$.	Write a multiplication example where one of the numbers ends in 0. _____ What is the product? _____
The breaking-apart algorithm you have learned is a good method for multiplying multidigit numbers in your head.	Multiply 20×38. $20 \times (30 + 8) = 600 + 160 = 760$	Find 45×21. First, write one factor as a sum. _____ Multiply by the other factor and add to calculate the product. _____

Unit 5, Lesson 13

YOUR TURN

Choose the Right Word

estimate estimation rounding

Fill in each blank with the correct word or phrase from the box.

1. Changing a number to the nearest ten or hundred is called _____.

2. To _____ is to give an answer that is close to the correct answer.

3. Using _____ can help you find an answer that is close to the correct answer.

Yes or No?

Answer these questions and be ready to explain your answers.

4. To easily estimate 46 × 70, should you round 46 to 50? _____

5. Is 1,200 a good estimate for 59 × 22? _____

6. Are the last two digits of the product 40 × 30 both zeros? _____

7. When using mental calculation to solve 38 × 19, do you have to break apart the smaller number to multiply? _____

Show That You Know

Use rounding to estimate each of the following products. Write the rounded expression and the estimate.

8. 18 × 33

9. 61 × 88

10. 47 × 10

11. 56 × 22

Find each product without writing out the multiplication.

12. 20 × 32 =

13. 30 × 25 =

14. 45 × 19 =

15. 22 × 55 =

Learn the Skill

Unit 5, Lesson 13

Learn the Skill

SOLVE on Your Own

Skills Practice

Remember that when you estimate, the answer does not need to be exact.

Use rounding to estimate each of the following products. Write the rounded expression and your estimate.

1. 10 × 67 _____

2. 14 × 39 _____

3. 82 × 18 _____

4. 29 × 14 _____

5. 11 × 12 _____

6. 16 × 82 _____

7. 36 × 29 _____

8. 87 × 55 _____

9. 97 × 11 _____

10. 23 × 495 _____

Find each product using mental calculation. Write your answer on the line.

11. 50 × 90 = _____

12. 17 × 30 = _____

13. 24 × 31 = _____

14. 15 × 80 = _____

15. 25 × 42 = _____

16. 12 × 39 = _____

17. 19 × 14 = _____

18. 65 × 11 = _____

19. 21 × 89 = _____

20. 82 × 99 = _____

Unit 5, Lesson 13

Choose a Strategy

Mental Calculation
Strategies
Try a Simpler Form of the Problem,
Make a Table or a Chart

Step 1: Read Jermaine recycles aluminum cans to earn extra money. On average, he collects enough cans to earn 20¢ per day. How could you quickly estimate the amount of money he would make after one month, six months, and one year?

STRATEGY	SOLUTION
Try a Simpler Form of the Problem There are an odd number of days in some months and one year. Rounding the number of days to a value that is easy to compute mentally will allow a quick estimation of the money earned.	**Step 2: Plan** Round the number of days in one month, six months, and one year to numbers that are multiples of 10. Multiply each by the amount earned every day. **Step 3: Solve** One month is between 28 and 31 days. Round to 30 days. Amount earned in one month = 30 × 20¢ = 600¢, or $6. Round six months to 180 days. 180 × 20¢ = 3,600¢, or $36. One year is 365 days. Round this number to 370 days. 370 × 20¢ = 7,400¢, or $74. **Step 4: Check** Since one year is twice as long as six months, the result of 7,400¢ ÷ 2 should be close to 3,600¢. 7,400¢ ÷ 2 = 3,700¢, so the estimate is close to the correct amount.
Make a Table or a Chart Once the amount earned in one month has been estimated, this value can be used to estimate the amount of money earned in other time periods.	**Step 2: Plan** Round the number of days in one month to 30, and use this to estimate the money earned in one month. Multiply this value by the number of months that cans are collected. Use a table to organize the information. **Step 3: Solve** Round one month to 30 days. Amount earned = 30 × 20¢ = 600¢. | Number of Months	Total Money Earned
1	600¢ or $6
6	600¢ × 6 = 3,600¢ or $36
12 (1 year)	600¢ × 12 = 7,200¢ or $72 | **Step 4: Check** Use division to check the multiplication. 600¢ ÷ 30 = 20¢; 3,600¢ ÷ 6 = 600¢; 7,200¢ ÷ 12 = 600¢

Choose a Strategy

YOUR TURN

Choose the Right Word

> multiples   rounding   table

Fill in each blank with the correct word or phrase from the box.

1. 110, 120, 1,000, and 1,000,000 are all _____ of 10.

2. Changing numbers by _____ to the nearest 10 is often used to estimate sums and products.

3. A _____ is used to arrange information in an organized way.

Yes or No?

Answer these questions and be ready to explain your answers.

4. Can the distributive property be used to multiply 30 × 14? _____

5. If factors in an expression are rounded, can they still be multiplied using the vertical algorithm? _____

6. Must a factor always be rounded up to estimate a product? _____

7. Is there only one way to estimate a product or sum? _____

Show That You Know

Estimate the product. Show how you rounded the numbers to find your estimate.

8. 9 × 11

   Expression:

   Estimate:

9. 261 × 19

   Expression:

   Estimate:

10. 335 × 45

    Expression:

    Estimate:

Estimate each product by using rounding and the distributive property.

11. 231 × 23

    Rounded expression:

    Distributive property:

    Estimate:

12. 445 × 13

    Rounded expression:

    Distributive property:

    Estimate:

13. 119 × 61

    Rounded expression:

    Distributive property:

    Estimate:

Reading Comprehension

READ on Your Own

Reading Comprehension Strategy: Text Structure

Transportation: Past to Future, pages 23–24

VOCABULARY
Watch for the words you are learning about.

expedition: a journey for a purpose, such as exploration

specimens: samples used to study or learn about something

vast: very large in size or amount

Fluency Tip
Identify words that you do not know. Find out how to pronounce them before reading.

Before You Read

Think about the story "In the Blink of an Eye." Why do you think someone would pay $14,000 to fly aboard the Concorde?

As You Read

Read "Harriman Goes to Alaska," pages 23–24. STOP

Think about the sequence of events throughout the article. Then number each event listed in the chart to show the sequence from first to last.

Events That Affected the Harriman Expedition	Order of Events
In the spring of 1899, Harriman invited a group of people to join him on an expedition to Alaska.	
When the boat returned to Seattle, it was filled with photographs, drawings, notes, and specimens.	
In early June, Harriman and a few others completed a 48-mile hike near Glacier Bay while looking for bears.	
The U.S. government bought Alaska from Russia for $7.2 million.	
They traveled in style by train from New York City to Seattle, Washington.	

After You Read

What kinds of transportation could you use today to get to Alaska?

_____

_____

Unit 5, Lesson 14

Problem Solving

SOLVE on Your Own

Transportation: Past to Future, page 25

Organize the Information

Read You Do the Math in the magazine. Then complete the following table with information on the total miles covered by each dogsled team.

Number of Days	1	2	3	4	5	6	7	8	9	10	11	12
Team #1 total miles	112				off					off		
Team #2 total miles	96			off				off				off
Team #3 total miles	84					off						

You Do the Math

Use the information in the table above to answer these questions. Write your answers in the space provided.

> Add the miles traveled each day rather than multiplying by the number of days.

1. Why might someone assume that Team #2 would win?

   _____
   _____
   _____

2. Which team would win the race? What advantages did this team have over other teams?

   _____
   _____
   _____

After You Solve

After learning some of the different factors involved in competing in a dogsled race, what strategy would you use to try and win the race? Explain.

_____
_____

54   Unit 5, Lesson 14

Solve It!

Application

The Four-Step Problem-Solving Plan

Step 1: Read	Step 2: Plan	Step 3: Solve	Step 4: Check
Make sure you understand what the problem is asking.	Decide how you will solve the problem.	Solve the problem using your plan.	Check to make sure your answer is correct.

Read the article below. Then answer the questions.

Fuel Cells

Today's cars run mostly on oil products such as gasoline. This fuel does not burn cleanly. It releases many harmful gases and particles into the air. One of the gases is carbon dioxide, CO_2. This is a greenhouse gas. A greenhouse gas traps heat near Earth's surface. Many scientists think carbon dioxide is the biggest reason for global warming. Global warming is an overall increase in the temperature on Earth.

Scientists are trying to find alternative fuels. A government program was founded in 2003. Its goal is to put fuel-cell powered cars on the road by the year 2020. Fuel cells make clean electrical power. They are quiet and cause very little pollution. A fuel cell changes hydrogen and oxygen into water. In the process, electricity is made. They give off only heat and water vapor. Water vapor is also a greenhouse gas, but it is much less damaging than CO_2. Using fuel cells may help to clean up the air.

1. How might the use of fuel cells help address pollution problems?
   _____
   _____
   _____

2. A town uses 613 gallons of imported oil every day. How many gallons of oil does the town use in a 30-day month?
   _____

Unit 5, Lesson 15   55

Application

YOUR TURN

Read the article below. Then answer the questions.

The Problems with Fuel Cells

While fuel cells offer many advantages, they still do have some problems. The biggest problem is their high cost. If fuel-cell cars cost much more to run than other types of cars, many people will not be able to make the change.

Suppose a gallon of gasoline costs $3. In order for fuel cells to be priced about the same, the energy they produce must cost $35 per kilowatt. A kilowatt is a unit of power equal to the power used by ten 100-watt light bulbs. Right now, people think that a fuel cell will cost about $110 per kilowatt. That would be similar to paying $9 for a gallon of gasoline.

Also, many of the parts that make up a fuel cell are expensive. One reason fuel cells cost so much is that they must use platinum, an expensive metal. Researchers are trying to find less expensive materials to use instead. If the cost can come down, people may be more willing to drive fuel-cell cars.

1. How do fuel-cell cars and gasoline-powered vehicles compare cost wise?

   _____

   _____

2. The projected price of a kilowatt of energy from a fuel cell is about how many times the desired price?

   _____

3. A fuel cell currently costs about $110 per kilowatt. If a person used 59 kilowatts of energy driving a car in a year, about how much would it cost? Show your rounded expression and your estimate.

   _____

   _____

Fluency Tip

Be careful to read every word without skipping or substituting words. If a sentence or paragraph does not make sense, read it again.

READ on Your Own

Reading Comprehension Strategy: Text Structure

Transportation: Past to Future, pages 26–28

VOCABULARY
Watch for the words you are learning about.

biodiesel: a fuel made from animal and vegetable fats

economy: the system in which a country's business and trade work together

pollute: to foul the land, air, or water

Fluency Tip
Skim the passage for words that are hard to pronounce. Practice reading those words ahead of time.

Before You Read

Consider what you learned about Edward Harriman in "Harriman Goes to Alaska." How might his expedition have been different from the average expedition?

As You Read

Read "Green Gas," pages 26–28.

In the flow chart below, describe the problems caused by gasoline. Then describe how using other types of fuel might be a solution.

The Problems
1. _____
2. _____

⬇

The Solutions
1. _____
2. _____
3. _____

After You Read

How might widespread use of other types of fuel or engines affect your life? Explain your answer.

_____

Unit 5, Lesson 15

Problem Solving

SOLVE on Your Own

Transportation: Past to Future, page 29

Organize the Information

Read the Math Project in the magazine. Then complete the table using information you have read. Round costs to the nearest cent.

To find the cost of fuel per mile, divide the fuel's cost per gallon by the car's mileage.

Type of Fuel	Cost of Car	Cost of Fuel per Mile	Total Miles per Year	Fuel Cost per Year	Total Cost of Car After 1 Year
gasoline			13,000		
ethanol			13,000		
biodiesel			13,000		
electricity			13,000		

Math Project

Use the information in the table above to answer these questions. Write your answers in the space provided.

1. What statements can you make about the cars for sale by looking at the table?
   _____
   _____

2. Which car would you decide to buy? Explain your reasoning.
   _____
   _____

3. If you drove more each year, would that change your decision about the car you would choose?
   _____
   _____

After You Solve

How else might you express the same information in the chart?
   _____

58   Unit 5, Lesson 15

Exponents

Learn the SKILL

Scientists often do experiments involving living cells. They can start with just one cell. This cell splits, or doubles, to make two cells. Then both cells double again to make four cells. The cells continue to double. If a scientist counts the cells after one cell has split five times, how many cells will there be?

VOCABULARY

Watch for the words you are learning about.

base: the number used as a factor in an expression with an exponent

cube: a number raised to the third power

exponent: a number that tells how many times a base is used as a factor; also called a power

square: a number raised to the second power

SKILL	EXAMPLE	WRITE AN EXAMPLE
A factor multiplied by itself can be written using a **base** and an **exponent.** The base is a factor and the exponent is the number of times the base is used as a factor. The exponent is sometimes referred to as the power.	$2 \times 2 \times 2 \times 2 \times 2 = 2^5$ In 2^5, the base is 2 and the exponent, or power, is 5.	Write an expression that can be represented using an exponent. _____ Name the base and the exponent. _____ _____

You simplify an expression with an exponent by multiplying the base by itself. The exponent gives the number of factors that will be multiplied.	Simplify 2^5.
	   Multiply 2 by itself 4 times.
	$2^5 = \underline{2 \times 2} \times 2 \times 2 \times 2$
	  $= \quad \underline{4} \times 2 \times 2 \times 2$
	  $= \qquad \underline{8} \times 2 \times 2$
	  $= \qquad\quad \underline{16 \times 2}$
	  $= \qquad\qquad 32$
		Simplify the expression you wrote above.
		
		_____

Raising a number to the second power is called finding the **square** of a number. Raising a number to the third power is called finding the **cube** of a number.	What is 4 squared? Four squared is four to the second power, or 4^2. $4^2 = 4 \times 4 = 16$ What is 4 cubed? Four cubed is four to the third power, or 4^3. $4^3 = 4 \times 4 \times 4 = 64$	Write a number and the square of the number. _____ What is the cube of your number? _____

Unit 5, Lesson 16

Learn the Skill

YOUR TURN

Choose the Right Word

> base   cube   exponent   square

Fill in each blank with the correct word or phrase from the box.

1. A(n) _____ tells how many times a number is used as a factor.

2. The _____ is the factor.

3. To _____ a number, multiply the number by itself.

4. To _____ a number you raise it to the third power.

Yes or No?

Answer these questions and be ready to explain your answers.

5. In the expression 2^3, is 3 the base? _____

6. In the problem $2^3 = 8$, is 2 the exponent? _____

7. Is the base the number that is being multiplied by itself? _____

8. Does the exponent give the number of times the number is multiplied by itself? _____

Show That You Know

Identify the base and the exponent.

9. $1^5 = 1$

   Base:

   Exponent:

10. $7^3 = 343$

    Base:

    Exponent:

11. $4^3 = 64$

    Base:

    Exponent:

Simplify each expression.

12. $1^8 =$

13. $7^2 =$

14. $4^4 =$

15. $5^3 =$

Represent these expressions with an exponent. Then write the value of the expression.

16. $8 \times 8 =$ _____ = _____

17. $12 \times 12 =$ _____ = _____

18. $10 \times 10 \times 10 =$ _____ = _____

SOLVE on Your Own

Skills Practice

> Remember, the exponent tells you how many times to multiply the base by itself.

Identify the base.

1. $1^6 = 1$ The base is _____.

2. $3^3 = 27$ The base is _____.

3. $8^2 = 64$ The base is _____.

Identify the exponent.

4. $5^5 = 3{,}125$ The exponent is _____.

5. $6^2 = 36$ The exponent is _____.

6. $9^3 = 729$ The exponent is _____.

7. $10^5 = 100{,}000$ The exponent is _____.

Simplify each expression.

8. $1^{112} = $ _____

9. $12^2 = $ _____

10. $8^3 = $ _____

11. $2^8 = $ _____

12. $0^{12} = $ _____

13. $3^4 = $ _____

14. $5^4 = $ _____

Unit 5, Lesson 16

Choose a Strategy

Exponents
Strategies
Draw a Picture or Use a Model, Find a Pattern

Step 1: Read In art class, Austin is making two square trays covered with square tiles. He wants to make a larger tray that has four times as many tiles as a smaller tray. One option he considers is shown at right. What are other possible sizes he could use for the smaller and larger trays?

STRATEGY	SOLUTION

Draw a Picture or Use a Model (area model)

Make square area models with equal numbers of rows and columns. Then make a table to record number of rows or columns and the total amount of squares in each area model. Multiply by four to find the size of the larger tray.

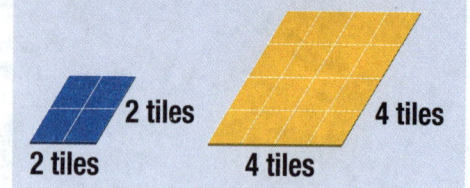

2 tiles × 2 tiles

4 tiles × 4 tiles

Step 2: Plan Create area models to model sizes for the smaller tray. Then use the table to find the possible sizes for the larger tray.

Step 3: Solve The specifics of each model are recorded below.

Number of Tiles in Each Row and Column	Total Tiles (Rows × Columns)	4 × Total Tiles
2	$2 \times 2 = 2^2 = 4$	$4 \times 4 = 16$
3	$3 \times 3 = 3^2 = 9$	$4 \times 9 = 36$
4	$4 \times 4 = 4^2 = 16$	$4 \times 16 = 64$
5	$5^2 = 25$	$4 \times 25 = 100$
6	$6^2 = 36$	$4 \times 36 = 144$
7	$7^2 = 49$	$4 \times 49 = 196$
8	$8^2 = 64$	$4 \times 64 = 256$
9	$9^2 = 81$	$4 \times 81 = 324$
10	$10^2 = 100$	$4 \times 100 = 400$

If the smaller tray is 3 tiles × 3 tiles, the larger tray is 6 tiles × 6 tiles. If the smaller tray is 4 tiles × 4 tiles, the larger tray is 8 tiles × 8 tiles. Other sizes are possible.

Step 4: Check Total tiles in the 6 tiles × 6 tiles tray is 36 tiles. Divide to check: 36 tiles ÷ 9 tiles is 4, so trays that are 6 tiles on each side and 3 tiles on each side work.

Find a Pattern

Make a list of squares of the whole numbers. If a tray has a certain number of tiles on a side, you square that number to find the total tiles in the tray. Look for a pattern that will make the total number of tiles four times as great.

Step 2: Plan Make a list of squares and look for a pattern.

Step 3: Solve List the squares of whole numbers:

1, 4, 9, 16, 25, 36, 49, 64, 81, 100

One pattern that helps to solve this problem is this:

4 × 1st square = 2nd square, so 1 and 2 work.

4 × 2nd square = 4th square, so 2 and 4 work.

4 × 3rd square = 6th square, so 3 and 6 work.

To find a size for the larger tray, double the length of smaller tray's sides.

Step 4: Check Use a calculator to test the pattern. 36 ÷ 9 = 16 ÷ 4 = 4 ÷ 1 = 4. This example follows the pattern.

YOUR TURN

Choose the Right Word

> base   cube   expression   factor

Fill in each blank with the correct word or phrase from the box.

1. $3^2 + 3^2$ is an example of a(n) _____.

2. To find the _____ of a number, raise the number to the third power.

3. In the equation, $3^2 = 9$, on the left side 3 is a _____ and 2 is a _____.

Choose a Strategy

Yes or No?

Answer these questions and be ready to explain your answers.

4. Is the value of 10^2 equal to 100? _____

5. Is $8^2 = 4^4$? _____

6. If you double the number of tiles on the side of a square, will the total number of tiles be twice as great? _____

7. If you divide the number of tiles on each side in half, will the total number of tiles be half as many? _____

Show That You Know

Simplify the following expressions. Find the value of the exponents first, and then do the operations.

8. $10^2 \div 5^2 =$

9. $3^2 + 4^2 - 5^2 =$

10. $3^2 \times 4 =$

11. $24^2 \div 12^2 =$

Write your answer to each exercise in the space provided.

12. $4 \times 6^2 =$

13. $14^2 \div 7^2 =$

14. $8^2 \div 4 =$

15. $18^2 \div 4 =$

Reading Comprehension

READ on Your Own

Reading Comprehension Strategy: Text Structure

Transportation: Past to Future, *pages 30–31*

VOCABULARY
Watch for the words you are learning about.

maintenance: people who keep something in good repair

Fluency Tip
Reread sentences that you find difficult. Change your expression as you read.

Before You Read

Think about the alternative fuel sources in "Green Gas." Which fuel source might you want to try out and why?

As You Read

Read "The Chunnel," pages 30–31. 🛑

Reread the first and fourth paragraphs on page 31. In the chart below, list the descriptive words in each paragraph. Then explain how the descriptive words helped you understand the paragraph.

Descriptive Words	How the Descriptive Words Helped Me Understand the Paragraph
First paragraph	
Fourth paragraph	

After You Read

What other modern-day structures can you think of that help people get from one place to another?

Unit 5, Lesson 17

SOLVE on Your Own

Transportation: Past to Future, page 32

Organize the Information

Read You Do the Math in the magazine. Use the information to complete the following table. Add to the table as needed to show more options.

Toll Booths Open	Toll Collectors				Radio Signals				Total
	Number of Booths	Cars per Minute (through each booth)	Total Cars Through Booths in 1 Minute		Number of Booths	Cars per Minute (through each booth)	Total Cars Through Booths in 1 Minute	Total Cars Through All Booths in 1 Minute
4	2	4	__ × 4 = 8	2	2	2 × 2 = __		
5								
6								

You Do the Math

Use the information in the table above to answer these questions. Write your answers in the space provided.

Listing possible answers may help you answer the magazine questions.

1. What pattern did you see in the data about the number of cars that can pass per minute through the booths using radio signals?
   _____
   _____

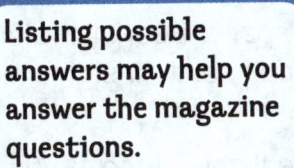

2. You used the Make a Table or a Chart strategy above. What other strategy could you use to solve this problem?
   _____

3. How many of each type of tollbooth do you think should be used? Explain your answer.
   _____

After You Solve

Why do you think some roads, bridges, and tunnels charge drivers tolls to use them?
   _____

Unit 5, Lesson 17

Application

Solve It!

The Four-Step Problem-Solving Plan

Step 1: Read	Step 2: Plan	Step 3: Solve	Step 4: Check
Make sure you understand what the problem is asking.	Decide how you will solve the problem.	Solve the problem using your plan.	Check to make sure your answer is correct.

Read the article below. Then answer the questions.

The Vacation of a Lifetime

Would the trip of your life be worth $100,000? For some, the answer is yes, if that trip's destination is space. Soon, travelers looking for a bigger thrill can set their sights higher, all the way into space.

The first space flights of the 1950s and 1960s did not make a full trip around Earth. Instead, they made suborbital flights. This means they exit Earth's atmosphere but do not go high enough to orbit the planet. This is the flight plan for the new space tourist. Such trips will go 62 miles above Earth. Once you are that high up, you can feel what it is like to be weightless.

Do you think these trips will be easy? Think again. People will be required to train like astronauts. They will learn how to move in different levels of gravity. They must know how to handle basic flight operations. They will also have life support training.

Two spaceports, like airports, have been planned to serve this new industry. One spaceport is planned for the United Arab Emirates and the other for Singapore.

1. What does suborbital travel offer that other vacations do not?

   _____
   _____
   _____

2. Suppose the lifespan of a suborbital space shuttle is 5,000 miles. Estimate how many suborbital round trips (to and from Earth) the shuttle can make.

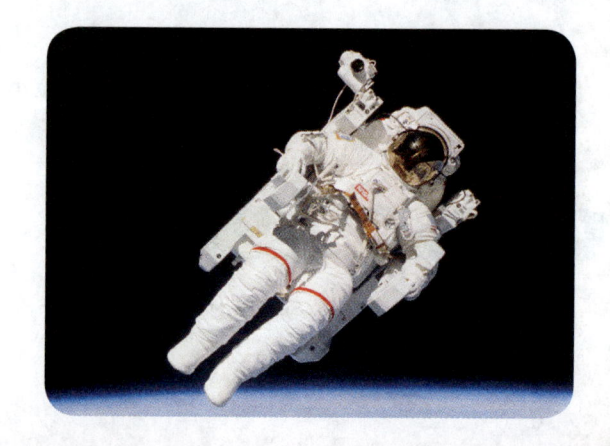

   _____
   _____

YOUR TURN

Application

Read the article below. Then answer the questions.

The Experience without the Travel

If you would like to have your space experience a little closer to home, there are many chances to do so. Companies have designed programs that imitate space travel in the safety of a NASA-type flight training session.

These flights take place aboard special airplanes. During take-off and landing, passengers are strapped into regular airplane seats but feel like they take off in a rocket. Once they are high enough, the plane begins a slow dive and passengers get to experience real space conditions. They feel the one-third gravity of Mars, and the one-sixth gravity experienced on the moon. Passengers are taught how to control their movements under these different conditions. They can also try zero gravity. In this session, passengers float about the airplane cabin, bouncing and bumping into each other.

It is a one-of-a-kind adventure. In the not too distant future, however, these low-gravity simulations may be replaced by real journeys into space. Are you up for the trip?

1. What can a space fantasy adventure teach you?
   _____
   _____
   _____

2. Because the moon has one-sixth the gravity of Earth, a person on the moon weighs one-sixth of his or her Earth weight. If someone weighs 180 pounds on Earth, how much would that person weigh on the moon?
   _____

3. The cruising speed for the plane that simulates weightlessness is about 17^2 mph. Simplify 17^2.
   _____

Fluency Tip
Change the expression in your voice to reflect whether information is surprising, serious, or descriptive.

Unit 5, Lesson 18

Reading Comprehension

READ on Your Own

Reading Comprehension Strategy: Text Structure

Transportation: Past to Future, pages 33–35

Fluency Tip
Remember to look up the meanings of unfamiliar words before you read.

Before You Read

Consider what you read about in "The Chunnel." Why is the Chunnel considered one of the wonders of the world?

As You Read

Read "Vacations in Space," pages 33–35. STOP

Complete the chart below by finding facts and opinions on the pages you just read.

Find This	What I Found
Find a fact about Yuri Gagarin on page 33.	
Find a fact about the International Space Station on page 34.	
Find a fact about space tourism on page 35.	

After You Read

What part of space travel do you think you would enjoy the most? Why?

68 Unit 5, Lesson 18

Problem Solving

SOLVE on Your Own

Transportation: Past to Future, *page 36*

Organize the Information

Read the Math Project in the magazine. Use the information to complete the following flowchart. Add to the chart as needed to show more options.

Round Trip to the Moon

Start at Earth	→	Travel to Moon	→	Stay on Moon	→	Travel to Earth
Distance = 0 Speed = 0		Distance = 240,000 mi Speed = _____ Time = _____		Distance = 0 Speed = 0 Time = _____		Distance = 240,000 mi Speed = _____ Time = _____

Total time for one round trip: _____

Math Project

Use the information in the flowchart above to answer these questions.
Write your answers in the space provided.

1. Why might there be more than one answer to the Math Project problem?

   _____
   _____

2. How much money would the company make each week? Explain your reasoning.

   _____
   _____
   _____
   _____

After You Solve

What would be another way to present the information in the flow chart above? How might this help solve the problem?

_____
_____

Unit 5, Lesson 18

Connections

Put It Together

Introducing Models to Represent Multidigit Division

You have learned how to multiply multidigit numbers. What is the product of 12 and 16? One way to get this answer is with repeated addition. The number 16 can be used as an addend 12 times or the number 12 can be used as an addend 16 times.

$16 + 16 + 16 + 16 + 16 + 16 + 16 + 16 + 16 + 16 + 16 + 16 = 192$

$12 + 12 + 12 + 12 + 12 + 12 + 12 + 12 + 12 + 12 + 12 + 12 + 12 + 12 + 12 + 12 = 192$

You have also learned an easier method: $12 \times 16 = 12(10 + 6) = 120 + 72 = 192$.

Division is the inverse of multiplication and can be solved by repeated subtraction. Every multiplication example has two related division problems.

Since $12 \times 16 = 192$, you can say $192 \div 16 = 12$ and $192 \div 12 = 16$. To find $192 \div 12$, simply count the number of times you can subtract 12 until you get to 0.

$192 - 12 - 12 - 12 - 12 - 12 - 12 - 12 - 12 - 12 - 12 - 12 - 12 - 12 - 12 - 12 - 12 = 0$

The answer is 16 because 12 was subtracted 16 times.

Practicing Using Models to Represent Multidigit Division

Use repeated subtraction to find each of the following quotients. Write your answer on the line.

1. $75 \div 15 = $ _____

2. $156 \div 12 = $ _____

3. $450 \div 50 = $ _____

4. $204 \div 17 = $ _____

5. $138 \div 23 = $ _____

YOUR TURN

Connections

Thinking About Models to Represent Multidigit Division

Think about the product of 10 × 24. You have learned the product of 10 and a number changes the place value of the number. The result is an additional 0 at the right of the number.
Examples: 10 × 24 = 240, 10 × 43 = 430, and 10 × 457 = 4,570.

Multiples of 10 will help you simplify the division example. Using multiples of 10 will help you divide more quickly. You will still do some subtraction.

736 ÷ 32 = □	32 × 10 = 320	
Subtract 320	736 − 320 = 416	10
Subtract 320 again	416 − 320 = 96	10
Subtract 32 × 3	96 − 96 = 0	+ 3
	answer :	23

Always remember to check your answer. If 736 ÷ 32 = 23, then 23 × 32 = 736.

Use what you have learned to answer the following questions.

1. Why do you think 320 was only subtracted twice?
   _____

2. If you used this method to calculate 736 ÷ 23, what number would you subtract first?
   _____

3. How many times could you subtract the number? _____

4. What is 736 ÷ 23? _____

5. What is the product of your answer and 23? _____

Tip When dividing larger numbers, you can also use multiplication and the Guess, Check, and Revise strategy to work the problem backwards.

Unit 5, Lesson 19

Connections

Show That You Know

Read the following scenario and use what you have learned about modeling division of multidigit numbers to answer the questions. Remember that you have two different methods to choose from.

> Mrs. Gallant is planning a summer vacation trip. She will drive 630 miles to get to her destination. She knows the following equation will help her figure out her speed, time, and distance traveled.
> speed (measured in miles per hour) × time (measured in hours) = distance (measured in miles)

The same division problem can be modeled in more than one way.

1. If you know how many hours Mrs. Gallant will drive, how can you find her average speed? (Hint: You can travel 120 miles in 2 hours at 60 miles per hour.)

2. If you know the number of miles Mrs. Gallant will drive and her average speed, how can you find the number of hours the trip will take?

3. How many hours will the trip take if she averages 63 miles per hour?

4. If the trip takes her 14 hours, what is her average speed?

Connections

Show That You Know (continued)

5. How many hours will the trip take if Mrs. Gallant's average speed is 70 miles per hour?

6. How many hours will the trip take if Mrs. Gallant's average speed is 35 miles per hour?

7. How are questions 5 and 6 related?

Review What You've Learned

8. What have you learned in this Connections lesson about the relationship between multiplication and division?

9. What have you learned in this Connections lesson that you did not already know?

10. How will this lesson help you divide multidigit numbers?

Unit 5, Lesson 19

Review and Practice

Skills Review

Multiply numbers in vertical form

Multiply the ones.
Add any regrouped tens.

$$\begin{array}{r}3\\68\\\times\ 24\\\hline 272\end{array}$$

Multiply the tens
and add the partial products.

$$\begin{array}{r}1\\68\\\times\ 24\\\hline 272\\+\ 1{,}360\\\hline 1{,}632\end{array}$$

Multiplying multidigit numbers

Multiply the ones.
Add any regrouped tens
and hundreds.

$$\begin{array}{r}4\ 3\\254\\\times\ 139\\\hline 2{,}286\end{array}\qquad\begin{array}{r}1\ 1\\254\\\times\ 139\\\hline 2{,}286\\7{,}620\end{array}$$

Multiply the tens
and add any regrouped
tens and hundreds.

$$\begin{array}{r}254\\\times\ 139\\\hline 2{,}286\end{array}$$

Multiply the hundreds
and add the partial products.

$$\begin{array}{r}7{,}620\\+\ 25{,}440\\\hline 35{,}306\end{array}$$

Mental calculation: Estimating products

Use rounding to estimate products or to check if your answer is reasonable.

$22 \times 67 = 1{,}474$. Is the answer reasonable?

Round 22 to 20 and round 67 to 70.

The estimated product is $20 \times 70 = 1{,}400$.
The answer is reasonable.

Mental calculation: Multiplying by multiples of 10

30×40 Use the basic fact: $3 \times 4 = 12$.

Add two zeros at the end of the product:

$30 \times 40 = 1{,}200$

Multiply mentally

Rewrite a number as a sum:

$30 \times 34 = 30 \times (30 + 4) = 900 + 120 = 1{,}020$

Numbers with exponents

$5^3 = 125$. In this equation, the base is 5 and the exponent is 3.

A square of a number is the number multiplied by itself.

A cube of a number is the number multiplied by itself twice.

Simplifying exponents

The exponent gives the number times the base is used as a factor.

$3^4 = 3 \times 3 \times 3 \times 3 = 81$

Strategy Review

- Use the distributive property to solve a simpler problem when multiplying multidigit factors. One of the factors can be written as a sum of two smaller numbers before multiplying. Choose combinations of addends that are easy to multiply by the other factor.

- To estimate a product of two multidigit numbers, find a simpler form of the problem by rounding one or both numbers to a value that is easy to compute.

- Looking for patterns of squares can help you find the relationships between two squared numbers.

Review and Practice

Skills and Strategies Practice

Complete the exercises below.

1. $24 \times 40 =$ _____
   $63 \times 21 =$ _____

2. Represent one factor as a sum and then multiply. More than one combination of addends may be correct.
   $22 \times 9 = ($ _____ $+$ _____ $) \times 9$
   $=$ _____ $+$ _____
   $=$ _____

3. Estimate the product of 73 and 59.
   _____

4. $40 \times 40 =$ _____
   $18 \times 20 = ($ _____ $\times 20) + ($ _____ $\times 20)$
   $=$ _____

5. $16^2 \div 8^2 =$ _____
   $20^2 =$ _____

6. 3^7 is the same as:
   _____

Test-Taking tip: When you study for a math test, review any formulas and example problems. Then practice the step-by-step procedures for solving problems. For example, review the steps in solving a multidigit multiplication problem using vertical form. Remember to add any regrouped tens and hundreds. Check your answer by breaking apart one addend. For 235×162, for example, you can solve in vertical format, and then check by multiplying 235×100 and adding the product to 235×62.

Unit 5, Lesson 20   75

Review and Practice

Unit Review

Circle the letter of the correct answer.

1. $10 \times 73 = $ _____

   A. 730   C. 800
   B. 750   D. 1,073

2. The estimated product of 33 and 21 is _____.

   A. 693   C. 500
   B. 600   D. 50

3. In the expression 7^{14}, 7 is the _____.

   A. exponent
   B. power
   C. base
   D. multiple

4. $70 \times 80 = $ _____

   A. 56   C. 5,600
   B. 560   D. 56,000

5. Estimate the product of 226×44.

   A. 800
   B. 8,000
   C. 80,000
   D. 800,000

6. $126 \times 245 = $ _____

   A. 30,670
   B. 30,840
   C. 30,870
   D. 32,870

7. $300 \times 30 = $ _____

   A. 900
   B. 1,000
   C. 9,000
   D. 90,000

8. $219 \times 219 \times 219 \times 219 = $ _____

   A. 219^2 C. 219^4
   B. 219^3 D. 219^5

9. The estimated product of 32 and 19 is _____.

   A. 6,080
   B. 6,000
   C. 608
   D. 600

10. $43 \times 11 = $ _____

    A. 473   C. 430
    B. 441   D. 484

11. $795 \times 162 = $ _____

    A. 128,690
    B. 128,780
    C. 128,790
    D. 128,800

12. $13 \times 49 = $ _____

    A. 588
    B. 516
    C. 637
    D. 529

Review and Practice

13. The expression 5 × 5 × 5 × 5 × 5 is the same as which of the following?

    A. 5^3
    B. 5^6
    C. 5^4
    D. 5^5

14. $4^5 =$ _____

    A. 16
    B. 64
    C. 256
    D. 1,024

15. 64 × 157 = _____

    A. 10,048
    B. 10,058
    C. 10,248
    D. 100,048

16. $3^2 \times 3^4 =$ _____

    A. 729
    B. 648
    C. 576
    D. 243

17. 160 × 82 = _____

    A. 1,312
    B. 13,020
    C. 13,120
    D. 131,200

18. $17^2 =$ _____

    A. 34
    B. 149
    C. 172
    D. 289

19. 22 × 22 = _____

    A. 442
    B. 484
    C. 444
    D. 462

20. 100 × 20 = _____

    A. 2
    B. 20
    C. 200
    D. 2,000

21. $4 \times 7^2 =$ _____

    A. 296
    B. 196
    C. 169
    D. 149

22. In the equation $3^2 = 9$, the base is _____.

    A. 9
    B. 2
    C. 3
    D. 3^2

23. The best estimation of 77 × 9 is _____.

    A. 90
    B. 720
    C. 880
    D. 900

24. $10^3 =$ _____

    A. 1,000
    B. 100
    C. 10
    D. 1

25. 27 × 51 = _____

    A. 1,350
    B. 1,351
    C. 1,375
    D. 1,377

Unit 5, Lesson 20

Unit 5 Reflection

MATH SKILLS

The easiest part about multiplying and dividing is

I can multiply and divide faster now because

MATH STRATEGIES & CONNECTIONS

The math strategies I found the most useful are

I can model multiplication and division using

READING STRATEGIES & COMPREHENSION

The easiest part about using text structure is

One way that text structure helps me with reading is

The vocabulary words I had trouble with were

INDEPENDENT READING

My favorite part of Transportation: Past to Future is

I read most fluently when

Transportation: Past to Future

UNIT 6
Two-Dimensional Shapes

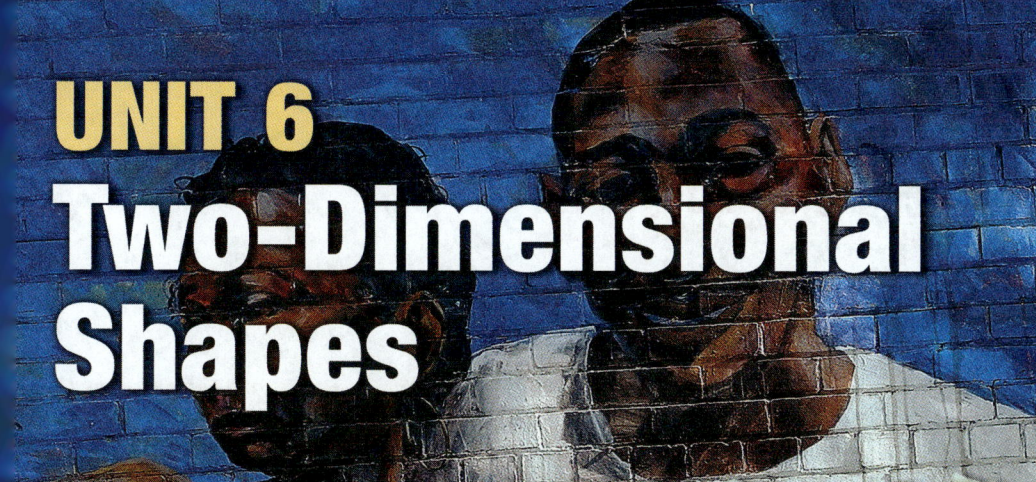

MATH SKILLS & STRATEGIES
After you learn the basic **SKILLS**, the real test is knowing when to use each **STRATEGY**.

AMP LINK MAGAZINE
You Do the Math and Math Projects: After you read each magazine article, apply what you know in real-world problems.
Fluency: Make your reading smooth and accurate, one tip at a time.

READING STRATEGY
Learn a variety of Visualizing techniques.

VOCABULARY
MATH WORDS:
Know them!
Use them!
Learn all about them!

CONNECTIONS
You own the math when you make your own connections.

Reading Comprehension Strategy

Reading Comprehension Strategy: Visualizing

How to Visualize

| **Use pictures** to help you visualize what the article does and does not tell you. | **Find descriptive and sensory words** and use them to form pictures in your mind of what you are reading. | **Draw conclusions** after forming pictures in your mind about what you are reading. | **Visualize a sequence** of events to help you understand what you are reading. | **Use visual aids** such as graphic organizers to help you understand what you are reading. |

You might be familiar with the saying "a picture is worth a thousand words." You can gather a lot of information by looking at a **picture.** Examine any pictures that go with what you read. Pictures help you understand what you are reading.

1. Murals are pictures or designs painted on buildings or walls. Look at the mural in the photograph to the left. What types of things do you see?

   _____
   _____
   _____
   _____
   _____

When there are no pictures, good readers create their own pictures by visualizing what they are reading. When you visualize, you make pictures in your mind. **Descriptive words** can help you make these pictures. These words often describe what we can see, hear, taste, smell, and feel.

Diego Rivera is known as "the Father of Mexican Mural Art." He was born in Mexico in 1886. He painted a lot and moved to Europe as a young man to study art. He wanted to paint pictures that showed the history of Mexico. He also wanted his pictures to be seen by many people.

2. If you were going to paint a mural on a wall, what would it look like? Write a short description of what you imagine and where you would paint it.

   _____
   _____
   _____
   _____
   _____

80   Unit 6

Reading Comprehension Strategy

When you read details, ask yourself, *What do these details suggest?* Use information in the paragraph, but also think about what you already know. **Drawing conclusions** will help you understand what the author means but does not say directly.

While he was in Europe, Diego Rivera saw that some Italian artists painted their scenes directly onto the walls of public places. Many of these colorful paintings covered whole walls and ceilings. Some showed crowds of people doing day-to-day things, such as working or cleaning. Others showed people celebrating or soldiers fighting. Still other paintings showed highly detailed designs and patterns. When Diego Rivera saw these paintings, he saw the future of Mexican art.	3. What conclusion can you draw about the Italian murals Diego Rivera saw? _____ _____ _____ _____ _____

When you visualize, notice how the author organizes details. For example, events might happen in order. When you **visualize a sequence,** you create a mental picture of each event, one after another. This can help you remember and understand what you are reading.

What Diego Rivera saw were murals, or paintings on walls. There are many kinds of murals. Some artists paint directly on the wall. Others paint the images in their studio on a large canvas and then hang the canvas on the wall. Still others use frescoes, where artists put plaster on a wall and then paint on the plaster. These are just a few of the many kinds of murals.	4. Think about what you have learned about Diego Rivera so far. What happened first? What happened next? _____ _____ _____

Another way to organize details is to **use visual aids.** Visual aids, such as graphic organizers, can help you break down the information into smaller pieces. You have read details about Diego Rivera in Europe. Now you will read about his return to Mexico. A Venn diagram can help you compare and contrast these details.

Diego Rivera moved back to Mexico in 1921. Not long after, he started painting murals that showed moments in Mexico's history and culture. He painted them mostly on the walls of public buildings so everyone could see them. Rivera's ideas influenced other Mexican painters, who also started painting murals. These painters were known as the Mexican Muralists.	5. On another sheet of paper, draw a Venn diagram. Use the left circle to write details about Diego Rivera in Europe, the right circle for details about Rivera in Mexico, and the middle for details that are true in both. _____ _____ _____

6. What types of details have helped you the most when you visualize?
_____
_____

7. How might you find more information to help you visualize something?
_____

Use the Strategies

Use the reading comprehension strategies you have learned to answer questions about the article below.

The Art of Roman Mosaics

A mosaic is a design formed by putting together small pieces. In ancient times, Romans made many pictures by cutting small pieces of stone and placing them next to each other. Each piece is a called a *tessera* (*tesserae* is the plural). Romans used tesserae made of natural materials, so the range of colors was limited.

A large Roman mosaic could take thousands of tesserae. Some Roman mosaics were based on geometric patterns. Differently shaped pieces were used to make the more complicated pictures. Artisans created lifelike images of animals, people, flowers, and trees out of these tiny pieces.

First, the design of the mosaic was drawn out. This took a long time because the artist had to think about the style, size, and message of the art. The mosaic might be a hunting scene or a scene from history. It might show a family. Many Roman mosaics featured gods and goddesses from mythology.

After the design was drawn and colored in, it went to craftsmen who would cut the tesserae. This was a long process. The pieces were cut from broken pieces of pottery and stone. Ironstone was used for red and brown. Limestone and sandstone were used for yellow and brown. Black and blue came from slate, and white came from chalk.

Each piece had to be fitted in cement by hand. The work required great patience and attention to detail. A mosaic that covered a rectangle measuring 15 feet by 9 feet contained about 120,000 pieces.

1. What do you predict this article will be about?
   _____
   _____
   _____

2. What descriptive words and phrases are used in the fourth paragraph?
   _____
   _____
   _____
   _____
   _____

3. Visualize a mosaic made from these tiles. Would the colors be bright? Why or why not?
   _____
   _____
   _____
   _____
   _____

4. What conclusion can you draw about how long it took to make a mosaic?
   _____
   _____
   _____
   _____
   _____

Use the Strategies

Reading Comprehension Strategies: Text Structure, Visualizing

Use the reading comprehension strategies you have learned in this and previous units to answer the questions below.

1. Visualize the process of making a mosaic. Explain the steps involved.
   _____
   _____

2. Which part of this article was hardest to understand? What strategies helped you understand this part?
   _____
   _____

Problem-Solving Strategies: Try a Simpler Form of the Problem; Guess, Check, and Revise

Use these problem-solving strategies to answer the questions below.

Marcia is going to make a design using three colors of stones. She will use an equal number of red stones, blue stones, and yellow stones.

3. Marcia decided to use 21 stones in all. She uses the Guess, Check, and Revise strategy to guess how many of each color she will use. She guesses that there will be eight of each stone. How could you check her guess?
   _____
   _____

4. Marcia now knows that eight stones of each color is not the correct answer. Should her next guess be more than or less than eight stones? Explain.
   _____
   _____

At first, it takes 30 seconds for Marcia to put down two pieces of stone in her mosaic. After the first 10 pieces, she needs to think more, so it takes her one minute to put down two stones.

5. How long will it take to put down all 21 stones? Explain how you can use the Try a Simpler Form of the Problem strategy to find the answer.
   _____
   _____
   _____
   _____

Unit 6

Learn the Skill

Two-Dimensional Shapes

Learn the SKILL

Sam, Tom, and Larissa are all playing catch. They are standing so that Sam throws to Tom, then Tom throws to Larissa, and then Larissa back to Sam. They are all standing 7 feet apart from each other. What shape do they form and what is the perimeter of this shape?

VOCABULARY

Watch for the words you are learning about.

congruent: exactly equal

polygon: a closed figure that is formed by three or more line segments that do not cross

quadrilateral: a polygon with four sides

regular polygon: a polygon with all angles and sides congruent

triangle: a polygon with three sides

SKILL	EXAMPLE	COMPLETE THE EXAMPLE
A **polygon** is a closed figure with at least three sides. A **triangle** has three sides. A **quadrilateral** has four sides. Here are the names for figures with five through 10 sides: Five sides: pentagon Six sides: hexagon Seven sides: heptagon Eight sides: octagon Nine sides: nonagon Ten sides: decagon	Which type of polygon do the friends form? There are three friends and they form three sides. The polygon they create is a triangle.	What is a polygon with five sides? _____
If all the sides and the angles of the polygon are **congruent,** then the polygon is considered to be a **regular polygon.**	Do the friends form a regular polygon? Yes. They are all standing the same distance from each other, so all the sides and angles are congruent.	If a triangle has sides of 6 feet, 2 feet, and 6 feet, is the triangle a regular polygon? _____
The perimeter of a polygon can be found by adding the lengths of all its sides.	What is the perimeter of the polygon formed by the friends? Each side is 7 feet and there are three sides. $7 + 7 + 7 = 21$ feet	What is the perimeter of a regular polygon with four sides? Each side is 2 feet. _____

YOUR TURN

Choose the Right Word

> congruent   polygon   perimeter   triangle

Fill in each blank with the correct word or phrase from the box.

1. If a polygon has three sides, then it is considered to be a _____.

2. If a shape is a regular polygon, then all the angles and sides are _____.

3. A _____ is a closed figure with three or more line segments that do not cross.

4. The _____ is the distance around a shape.

Yes or No?

Answer these questions and be ready to explain your answers.

5. Is a triangle with sides of 3 feet, 3 feet, and 3 feet a regular polygon? _____

6. If there was a regular polygon with four sides and one side was 2 feet long, would the perimeter be equal to 8 feet? _____

7. To find the perimeter of a quadrilateral, can you add only two sides? _____

8. If all the sides are congruent, can one side be smaller than another? _____

Show That You Know

What shape does the number of sides describe? Write your answer on the line.

9. Six sides

10. Four sides

11. Three sides

Find the perimeter of each shape, given the sides below. Write your answer on the line.

12. 3 feet, 2 feet, 2 foot

13. 4 feet, 4 feet, 4 feet, 4 feet

14. 3 feet, 1 foot, 1 foot, 1 foot, 1 foot

15. 7 feet, 4 feet, 5 feet

Unit 6, Lesson 1

Learn the Skill

SOLVE on Your Own

Skills Practice

> Remember, the sides of a regular polygon are all the same length.

The lengths of the sides of polygons are given. For each, write the name of the type of polygon described, the perimeter of the polygon, and whether or not the shape is a regular polygon.

1. 4 feet, 4 feet, 4 feet _____

2. 6 feet, 7 feet, 6 feet, 7 feet, 6 feet, 7 feet _____

3. 5 feet, 5 feet, 5 feet, 5 feet, 5 feet _____

4. 1 foot, 1 foot, 1 foot, 1 foot, 1 foot, 1 foot, 1 foot, 1 foot _____

5. 3 feet, 4 feet, 3 feet, 5 feet _____

6. 7 feet, 9 feet, 3 feet, 3 feet _____

7. 12 feet, 15 feet, 23 feet, 12 feet, 12 feet, 5 feet, 16 feet _____

8. 21 feet, 29 feet, 31 feet _____

9. 17 feet, 17 feet, 17 feet, 17 feet _____

10. 21 feet, 22 feet, 23 feet, 24 feet, 25 feet _____

Choose a Strategy

Two-Dimensional Shapes

Strategy
Draw a Picture or Use a Model

Step 1: Read Your class is having an art party. Poster board needs to be hung on the walls all around the room to use for drawing and painting. First, you need to find the perimeter of the room. You can measure three sides of the room (30 ft, 45 ft, 30 ft), but part of the back wall is blocked by heavy boxes. How can you still find the classroom's perimeter?

STRATEGY	SOLUTION
Draw a Picture or Use a Model Polygons are simple figures. They are usually easy to draw. If you draw a polygon, you can clearly see it and easily identify it. Use the drawing to find the missing measurements.	**Step 2: Plan** Draw a picture of the room and label the lengths of its sides. Then identify the polygon and use what you know to find the length of the back wall. **Step 3: Solve** Back wall 30 ft 30 ft 45 ft The shape of the classroom looks like a rectangle. The opposite sides of a rectangle are equal in length. The length of the missing side must be 45 feet. That makes the perimeter 30 ft + 45 ft + 30 ft + 45 ft = 150 ft. **Step 4: Check** You can subtract to check your addition. 150 − 30 − 45 − 30 − 45 = 0
Draw a Picture or Use a Model Many common objects are shaped like polygons. For example, a piece of paper is a rectangle, the side of a pyramid is a triangle, and a stop sign is an octagon.	**Step 2: Plan** Identify the shape of the room. Then use an object of the same shape to help you determine the length of the back wall. **Step 3: Solve** The room is shaped like a rectangle. A piece of paper is also a rectangle. The sides of the piece of paper are 8.50 inches, 11 inches, 8.50 inches, and 11 inches. Opposite sides are equal. You can assume the same for the room. That makes the perimeter 30 ft + 45 ft + 30 ft + 45 ft = 150 ft. **Step 4: Check** Use blocks to build a model of a rectangle. Count the blocks that make up opposite sides to check that they are equal.

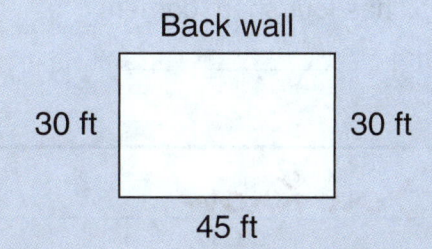

Choose a Strategy

YOUR TURN

Choose the Right Word

> octagon   pentagon   rectangle

Fill in each blank with the correct word or phrase from the box.

1. A(n) _____ has only five sides.

2. If you look at a stop sign, you may notice that it is in the shape of a(n) _____.

3. The side of a box has four sharp corners and looks like a(n) _____.

Yes or No?

Answer these questions and be ready to explain your answers.

4. Are all regular polygons congruent? _____

5. Do some real-world objects look like polygons? _____

6. Would a postcard have the shape of a triangle? _____

7. Would you add six numbers to find the perimeter of a hexagon? _____

Show That You Know

Identify the two-dimensional shape that matches each object.

8. a $10 bill

9. the head of an arrow

10. the wheel of a bus

11. a CD case

12. a kite

Choose an everyday object that could model the shapes below.

13. rectangle

14. quadrilateral

15. triangle

16. octagon

Unit 6, Lesson 2

Reading Comprehension

READ on Your Own

Reading Comprehension Strategy: Visualizing

Artworks, pages 3–4

Before You Read

Visualize drawings, paintings, or other art projects that you have made. What kinds of shapes did you use to represent objects?

As You Read

Read "Cubism," pages 3–4. 🛑

Think about what you have learned in this article about cubism. Choose an image in the magazine and examine it carefully.

How did the artist show a curve?

_____
_____

Is the image you chose a good example of cubism? Why or why not?

_____
_____
_____

In the space below, draw a dog's face using geometric shapes.

After You Read

What types of objects do you think would be easy to show in a cubist painting? Explain.

_____
_____

VOCABULARY

Watch for the words you are learning about.

abstraction: an artistic style in which objects are simplified or changed rather than shown realistically

collage: an artwork made up of cut or torn materials glued to a flat surface

cubism: a style of art in which natural forms are shown as geometric shapes

Fluency Tip

Use periods, commas, question marks, and exclamation points to tell you when to pause.

Unit 6, Lesson 2

Problem Solving

SOLVE on Your Own

Artworks, page 5

Organize the Information

Read You Do the Math in the magazine. Then complete the table below to show the number of sides for different kinds of polygons.

Number of Sides	Polygon
3	triangle
4	
5	
6	
8	

Remember what you have learned about quadrilaterals and triangles. It will help you with your drawing.

You Do the Math

Use the table above to help you calculate the number of sides in your drawing. Make your drawing on a separate sheet of paper. Then use your drawing and the table to answer the questions below.

1. How could you estimate the number of sides in your drawing before you count them?

   _____

   _____

2. Imagine that your drawing had 10 shapes and 56 sides. What would you do to fix it?

   _____

   _____

After You Solve

What objects do you think would be the most difficult to represent with polygons?

_____

_____

Unit 6, Lesson 2

Angles

Learn the SKILL

As Sophie is walking downtown, she looks at the buildings and notices they are made up of different angles. She wonders if the angles have specific names. She also wonders how big the angles are. How can she name and measure them?

VOCABULARY

Watch for the words you are learning about.

acute angle: an angle with a measure between 0° and 90°

angle: a figure made up of two rays or sides with a common endpoint

obtuse angle: an angle with a measure greater than 90° and less than 180°

ray: a part of a line, beginning at an endpoint and continuing in one direction with no end

right angle: an angle with a measure of 90°

straight angle: an angle with a measure of 180°

vertex: the point at which two sides of an angle meet

SKILL	EXAMPLE	COMPLETE THE EXAMPLE
All **angles** are measured in degrees. An **acute angle** is one that is between 0° and 90°, whereas an **obtuse angle** is greater than 90° and less than 180°.	An angle has a measurement of 45°. What type of angle is it? It is an acute angle. It is between 0° and 90°.	An angle has a measurement of 145°. What type of angle is it? _____
A **right angle** has a measurement of 90° exactly. A **straight angle** has a measurement of 180°. It looks like a straight line.	An angle has a measurement of 180°. What type of angle is it? It is a straight angle.	An angle has a measurement of 90°. What type of angle is it? _____
A protractor can be used to measure an angle. Place the center of the protractor at the **vertex**. Line one **ray** up with the 0° line on the protractor. The point that the other ray extends to shows the measurement of the angle.	Measure the angle. What type of angle is it? 35°; It is an acute angle.	Measure the angle. What type of angle is it? _____

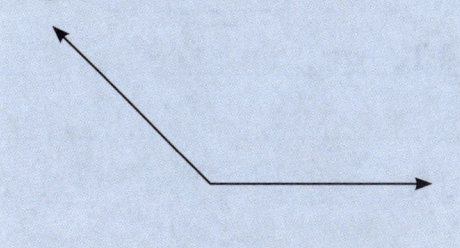

Unit 6, Lesson 3

Learn the Skill

YOUR TURN

Choose the Right Word

> acute angle   angle   obtuse angle
> right angle

Fill in each blank with the correct word or phrase from the box.

1. An angle that measures 90° is called a(n) _____.

2. When two rays meet at a vertex, they form a(n) _____.

3. A(n) _____ is greater than 90°.

4. A(n) _____ is less than 90°.

Yes or No?

Answer these questions and be ready to explain your answers.

5. If there is a straight line, could that be considered an angle? _____

6. Is an angle acute if it is 95°? _____

7. Is a right angle the same as an angle that is 90°? _____

8. Could an angle with a measurement of 45° be obtuse? _____

Show That You Know

State whether the angle is acute, obtuse, right, or straight.

9. 77° *acute*

10. 137° *obtuse*

11. 178° *obtuse*

12. 90° *right*

13. 2° *acute*

14. 85° *acute*

15. ⟷ *straight*

SOLVE on Your Own

Skills Practice

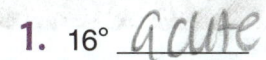

Remember, an acute angle is less than 90°, a right angle is 90°, and an obtuse angle is greater than 90°.

State whether the angle is acute, obtuse, right, or straight.

1. 16° _acute_
2. 68° _acute_
3. 180° _straight_
4. 169° _obtuse_
5. 125° _obtuse_
6. 100° _obtuse_
7. 90° _right_
8. 45° _acute_
9. 72° _acute_
10. 65° _acute_
11. 97° _obtuse_
12. 118° _obtuse_

Measure the following angles with a protractor.

13. _____

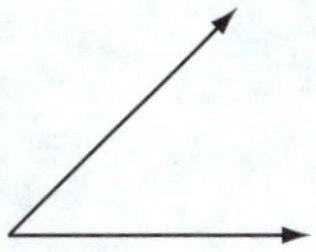

14. _____

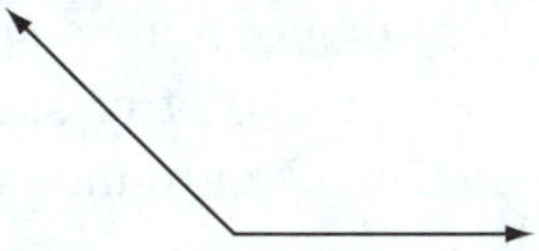

15. _____

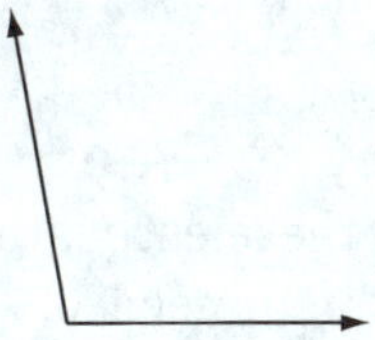

16. _____

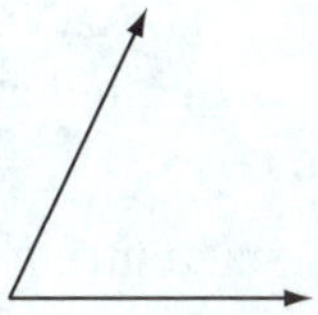

Unit 6, Lesson 3   93

Choose a Strategy

Angles
Strategies
Draw a Picture or Use a Model;
Guess, Check, and Revise

Step 1: Read A birdhouse hangs in your yard. The front is shaped like a pentagon. You want to tell a friend the approximate measurement of the angles so she can get a good idea of what it looks like. How can you estimate the measurement of those angles?

STRATEGY	SOLUTION
Draw a Picture or Use a Model The face of a clock is a good model for estimating the measure of different angles. At noon the angle made by the clock hands is 0°. At three o'clock it is 90°. At six it is 180°.	**Step 2: Plan** Use the face of a clock as a model to estimate the angles of the birdhouse. The birdhouse has the following shape: **Step 3: Solve** Use two sticks to model clock hands. Hold them together to show 3 o'clock. Then hold the sticks up to the angles of the birdhouse and compare. Two of the angles (at the bottom) should be around 90°, two should be slightly more than 90°, and one (at the top) should be around half of 90°, or 45°. **Step 4: Check** Use a protractor to measure the angles of the birdhouse.
Guess, Check, and Revise You can estimate the measures of the angles using multiples of 45°. A 45° angle is half the size of a 90° angle. Then you can use the estimates to draw the shape.	**Step 2: Plan** Make initial estimates using multiples of a 45° angle. Use these estimates to draw a picture, and revise the estimates and picture if needed. **Step 3: Solve** The smallest angle (at the top) is close to a 45° angle. Two of the angles are close to 90° angles. Guess 135° for the remaining angles. These measurements do not look correct in a drawing. Revise the guess to between 135° and 180°. **Step 4: Check** Use a protractor to measure the angles of the birdhouse and compare the measurements to the angles on your drawing.

YOUR TURN

Choose the Right Word

> protractor   right angle   straight angle

Fill in each blank with the correct word or phrase from the box.

1. Angles can be measured or drawn using a _____.

2. When it is 3 o'clock, clock hands show a _____.

3. A _____ is shown by the hands of a clock when it is 6 o'clock.

Choose a Strategy

Yes or No?

Answer these questions and be ready to explain your answers.

4. Must the peak of a roof always be an acute angle? _____

5. Can the hands of a clock be used to show an angle greater than 180? _____

6. If you added a right angle and an acute angle together, would the new angle be obtuse? _____

7. A tree has grown crooked. Could the angle formed at its base measure 85°? _____

Show That You Know

Identify the type of angle formed by the hands of a clock.

8. 2:00

9. 4:00.

10. 1:30

11. 1:20

Estimate the measure of the angle formed by the hands of a clock.

12. 2:00

13. 5:00

14. 1:30

15. 4:00

Unit 6, Lesson 4   95

Reading Comprehension

READ on Your Own

Reading Comprehension Strategy: Visualizing

Artworks, pages 6–7

VOCABULARY

Watch for the words you are learning about.

graffiti: writing or drawing on a public surface

vandalism: damage to someone else's property

Fluency Tip

Change the expression in your voice to reflect whether information is surprising, serious, or descriptive.

Before You Read

Think about what you read in "Cubism." Do you think angles play an important role in cubist art? Explain.

As You Read

Read "Murals," pages 6–7. 🛑

Reread "Graffiti" on page 7. Then complete the chart below. Use the chart to help you draw a conclusion and visualize what you read.

Details about graffiti:
- illegal because it is done without permission
  _____
  _____
  _____

My personal experience:
  _____
  _____

My conclusion:
  _____
  _____
  _____

After You Read

Explain the difference between a mural and graffiti painted on the side of a building.
_____
_____

96   Unit 6, Lesson 4

Problem Solving

SOLVE on Your Own

Artworks, page 8

Organize the Information

Read You Do the Math in the magazine. Sketch the design for your mural on a separate sheet of paper. Then complete the following table by describing the location of each angle and its measure.

Right Angles	Acute Angles	Obtuse Angles
book corners, 90°		

You Do the Math

Use your drawing and the information in the table above to answer these questions. Write your answers in the space provided.

Visualizing angles in nature may help you answer the magazine questions.

1. Which type of angle was easiest to include in your drawing? Why do you think this is?

   _____
   _____

2. Which angle was hardest to include in your drawing? Why?

   _____
   _____

After You Solve

Imagine you are sitting near a stream in the woods. Describe where you might see a right angle, an acute angle, and an obtuse angle in this scene.

_____
_____

Unit 6, Lesson 4

Application

Solve It!

The Four-Step Problem-Solving Plan

Step 1: Read	Step 2: Plan	Step 3: Solve	Step 4: Check
Make sure you understand what the problem is asking.	Decide how you will solve the problem.	Solve the problem using your plan.	Check to make sure your answer is correct.

Read the article below. Then answer the questions.

M. C. Escher

Is it possible to draw an impossible shape? M. C. Escher, an artist born in the Netherlands in 1898, knew how.

One of his famous paintings is called *Ascending and Descending.* It shows people on the square top of a building. Each edge of the square is a staircase. The people are all walking up. Since there is no break on the roof, the staircase does not appear to end. Once the people have walked completely around the square, they do not appear to be higher. Yet they are always going up the stairs. So how did Escher do it? He used distance perspective to make some sides appear higher than they should be and some sides appear lower than they should be.

The picture *Belvedere* features another of his impossible buildings. The building is composed of a rectangular floor and roof, and four columns along each long edge. The strange part is, all of the columns seem to go straight up but some actually go to the opposite side.

1. These books are the same, but one book has been tilted away from you.
   Which angle, x or y, appears to be a right angle?

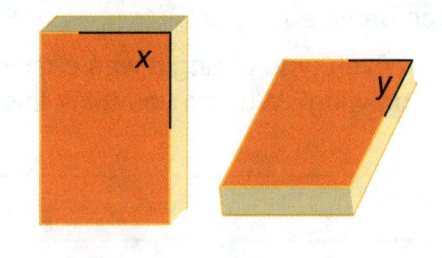

   _____

2. Why do angle x and angle y appear to be different, even though they are both the same corner on identical books?

   _____
   _____
   _____

YOUR TURN

Application

Read the article below. Then answer the questions.

Changing Shapes

M. C. Escher was a master at changing shapes. One of his works was called *Metamorphosis III*. The word metamorphosis means "a change or transformation." Only a part of *Metamorphosis III* is shown here. Escher started with black and white squares on the left side. As he moved to the right, he changed the squares to other quadrilaterals and then into bees. In the drawing, he included lizards, fish, geese, and boats, all transforming from one shape to another. At the end, he draws a small town that changes into a chessboard.

The polygons that Escher used in *Metamorphosis III* included squares, quadrilaterals, triangles, and hexagons. How did he change a square into a triangle? He shortened one side more and more until it became a point. He made the changes a little at a time so it seemed smooth. All in all, you would have to say that Escher was a good student of geometry.

Fluency Tip
Identify words that you do not know. Find out how to pronounce them before reading.

1. What are some of the things Escher drew in *Metamorphosis III*?
   _____
   _____

2. Look at the image above. How do the shapes change as you move your eye along the page from top to bottom?
   _____
   _____
   _____
   _____

3. In the image above, do the changes seem smooth? How might the artist make the shapes seem to flow together more smoothly?
   _____
   _____

Unit 6, Lesson 5   99

Reading Comprehension

READ on Your Own

Reading Comprehension Strategy: Visualizing

Artworks, pages 9–11

VOCABULARY

Watch for the words you are learning about.

contrast: in art, the difference between the darkest and brightest areas

optical: related to the eye or to seeing

Fluency Tip

As you read and reread, pay attention to punctuation marks that are clues to correct phrasing.

Before You Read

Think about what you read in "Murals." Do you think graffiti should be considered art? Why or why not?

As You Read

Read "Op Art," pages 9–11.

Look at the pictures in the article to help you visualize what the article is telling you. Explain how each artist created an optical illusion.

Image: page 9

_____

_____

Image: page 10

_____

_____

Image: page 11

_____

_____

After You Read

What other art are you familiar with that uses optical illusions?

_____

_____

_____

100 Unit 6, Lesson 5

Problem Solving

SOLVE on Your Own

Artworks, page 12

Organize the Information

The lines below form a checkerboard. The table shows the pattern between the number of lines and the number of spaces between the lines. Complete the table to show the pattern. Then make a table like the one below to organize the pattern you find in your own drawing for You Do the Math in the magazine.

Lines	Spaces	Increase
4	1	none
6	4	3
8	9	5
10	16	
12		
14		
16		
18		
20		

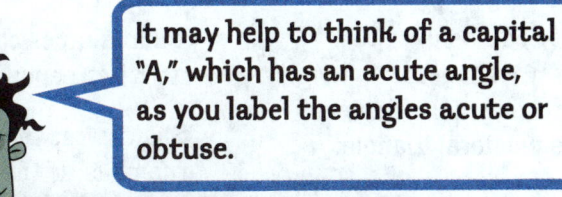

It may help to think of a capital "A," which has an acute angle, as you label the angles acute or obtuse.

Math Project

Use your drawing and the information in the table above to answer these questions. Write your answers in the space provided.

1. What was the best way to avoid making a right angle?
   _____

2. When two lines intersect, how many angles are formed? Is there a pattern to the angles?
   _____
   _____

After You Solve

What polygons are formed in your design?
_____

Unit 6, Lesson 5   101

Learn the Skill

Describing and Classifying Shapes Using Sides and Angles

Learn the SKILL

Shawna has four pencils. All of her pencils are the same length. How many different kinds of triangles or quadrilaterals can she make with those pencils?

VOCABULARY

Watch for the words you are learning about.

equilateral triangle: a triangle with three congruent sides

isosceles triangle: a triangle with at least two congruent sides

parallelogram: a quadrilateral with both pairs of opposite sides parallel

rectangle: a parallelogram with four right angles

rhombus: a parallelogram with four congruent sides

scalene triangle: a triangle with no congruent sides

similar: same in shape but different in size

square: a quadrilateral with four right angles and four congruent sides

trapezoid: a quadrilateral with one pair of opposite sides parallel

SKILL	EXAMPLE	COMPLETE THE EXAMPLE
Sides can be used to classify shapes. A triangle with congruent sides is an **equilateral triangle**. A triangle with no congruent sides is a **scalene triangle**. A **parallelogram** with all sides congruent is a **rhombus**. A **square** is one type of rhombus. A **trapezoid** is a quadrilateral with only two sides parallel.	What shapes can Shawna make with her pencils? She can make square or a different rhombus. If the angles are all the same then it is a square. Otherwise, it is a rhombus. What shape could Shawna make with two and a half pencils? Shawna could make an **isosceles triangle.**	A quadrilateral has one pair of opposite sides that are parallel. What is it called? _____
Angles also help classify a shape. A triangle with all angles equal is an equilateral triangle. A quadrilateral with all angles equal is a **rectangle**. Two shapes of the same type but with different sizes are called **similar**.	Bob walks from his house to school. Then he walks the same distance from school to John's house. Then he walks the same distance from John's house back home. If Bob created the same angle each time he went to a new location, what shape is the path he walked? The shape is an equilateral triangle.	A parallelogram has all right angles. The sides are not congruent. What is the shape called? _____

YOUR TURN

Choose the Right Word

> equilateral   rectangle   rhombus
> square   trapezoid

Fill in each blank with the correct word or phrase from the box.

1. If all the angles in a quadrilateral are congruent, but the sides are not congruent, then the shape is a(n) _____.

2. A(n) _____ triangle has sides that are all the same length.

3. A quadrilateral with one pair of parallel sides is a(n) _____.

4. A parallelogram that is both a rhombus and a rectangle is a(n) _____.

Yes or No?

Answer these questions and be ready to explain your answers.

5. Can an isosceles triangle have all equal angles? _____

6. Is a square a parallelogram? _____

7. Can a square also be considered a rectangle? _____

8. Can all the angles of a square be equal to 95°? _____

9. Can a quadrilateral and a triangle be similar? _____

Learn the Skill

Show That You Know

Name the type of polygon described.

10. Three sides, two sides equal

11. Four sides, two sides parallel, two sides not parallel

12. Four sides, all right angles

13. Three sides, all sides congruent

14. Four congruent sides

15. Three sides, 3 feet, 4 feet, and 6 feet long

16. A quadrilateral with opposite sides parallel

Unit 6, Lesson 6   103

Learn the Skill

SOLVE on Your Own

Skills Practice

Remember what you have learned about polygons. Try drawing the shape to help you visualize it.

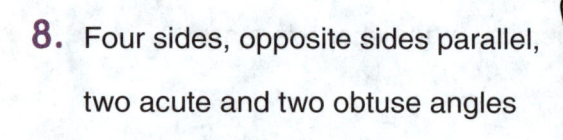

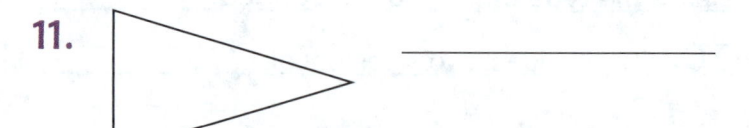

Name the type of polygon described. If it is not a polygon, write "NP."

1. Two sides _____

2. Three sides, none congruent _____

3. Two sets of parallel sides, all sides congruent, obtuse and acute angles _____

4. One side _____

5. A parallelogram with all right angles, opposite sides congruent _____

6. Four congruent sides, all right angles _____

7. Three sides, all equal to 6 feet _____

8. Four sides, opposite sides parallel, two acute and two obtuse angles _____

9. Three sides, lengths 8 feet, 8 feet, and 2 feet _____

10. _____

11. _____

12. _____

13. _____

104   Unit 6, Lesson 6

Describing and Classifying Shapes Using Sides and Angles

Strategies

Make a Table or a Chart, Draw a Picture or Use a Model

Step 1: Read Gannon goes to the park and sees many kites in the sky. The shapes of the kites include equilateral triangles, isosceles triangles, rectangles, and trapezoids. He says all the kites have parallel sides and acute angles. Is he correct?

STRATEGY	SOLUTION
Make a Table or a Chart Making a table of shapes and their sides and angles can be a good way to organize the information.	**Step 2: Plan** Make a table of the shapes Gannon sees in the sky. Then check to see if he is correct. **Step 3: Solve** | Polygon	Parallel Sides?	Acute Angles?
---	---	---
equilateral triangle	no	yes
isosceles triangle	no	at least two
rectangle	yes	no
trapezoid	yes	at least one	 Gannon is wrong. The triangles do not have parallel sides. Also, the rectangle has no acute angles. **Step 4: Check** Cut shapes out of paper to match Gannon's kites. Compare the sides and angles with information from the chart.
Draw a Picture or Use a Model Instead of making a table, you can also draw all the possible shapes. Then you can see which shapes have parallel sides, and estimate their angle measures.	**Step 2: Plan** Draw pictures of the shapes of the kites in the sky. Use those pictures to help you determine if Gannon is correct. **Step 3: Solve** isosceles triangle equilateral triangle rectangle trapezoid Gannon is wrong. The triangles do not have parallel sides. Also, the rectangle has no acute angles. **Step 4: Check** Use the definitions to make sure you have drawn the correct polygons.

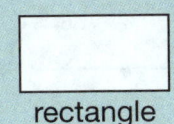

Choose a Strategy

Unit 6, Lesson 7

Choose a Strategy

YOUR TURN

Choose the Right Word

> equilateral triangle   isosceles triangle
> rhombus   trapezoid

Fill in each blank with the correct word or phrase from the box.

1. The three angles in a(n) _____ _____ are congruent.

2. A(n) _____ has four sides of equal length.

3. A(n) _____ has two sides that are congruent.

4. If a polygon has four sides but only two are parallel, it is a(n) _____.

Yes or No?

Answer these questions and be ready to explain your answers.

5. Can a rhombus also be a trapezoid? _____

6. Can a rectangle be a trapezoid? _____

7. If a triangle has three congruent angles, can it be both equilateral and isosceles? _____

8. Can a right triangle be scalene? _____

Show That You Know

Make a sketch of the following shapes.

9. isosceles triangle

10. rhombus

Describe each of the following.

11. the sides of a scalene triangle

12. the angles of a rectangle

13. the sides of a rhombus

14. the sides of an equilateral triangle

Reading Comprehension

READ on Your Own

Reading Comprehension Strategy: Visualizing

Artworks, pages 13–14

VOCABULARY

Watch for the words you are learning about.

relief sculpture: a type of art in which the image is raised off the background surface

sculptures: three-dimensional artworks that are carved, cast, assembled, or modeled into hard surfaces

Fluency Tip

Be careful to read every work without skipping or substituting words. If a sentence does not make sense, reread every word.

Before You Read

Think about what you read in "Op Art." What projects have you made that might be considered op art?

As You Read

Read "Sculpture," pages 13–14. 🛑

Then complete the concept map to organize information about different methods for making sculptures.

- Carving is cutting away from a material, such as clay, ice, food, wax, soap, or rock.
- Assembling
- Casting
- Modeling

(Sculpting Methods)

After You Read

What method or methods have you used to create sculptures? Describe how you used the methods.

_____

_____

Unit 6, Lesson 7 107

Problem Solving

SOLVE on Your Own

Artworks, page 15

Organize the Information

Read You Do the Math in the magazine. Then complete the table below with information on the number of acute and obtuse angles for each polygon.

Polygon	Number of Acute Angles	Number of Obtuse Angles	Total Number of Angles
equilateral triangle	3	0	3
trapezoid			
rhombus			
regular hexagon			

You Do the Math

Use the information in the table above to answer these questions. Write your answers in the space provided.

1. How could you cover the shape with the greatest and fewest number of tiles?

   _____
   _____

Making sketches of the different polygons will help you answer the magazine questions.

2. Which shape of tile would require the greatest number of gold nails? Which would require the greatest number of silver nails?

   _____
   _____
   _____

After You Solve

Why would you not use square tiles or rectangular tiles for this project?

_____
_____

108   Unit 6, Lesson 7

Solve It!

Application

The Four-Step Problem-Solving Plan

Step 1: Read	Step 2: Plan	Step 3: Solve	Step 4: Check
Make sure you understand what the problem is asking.	Decide how you will solve the problem.	Solve the problem using your plan.	Check to make sure your answer is correct.

Read the article below. Then answer the questions.

The Start of Dadaism

In 1916, a group of artists, writers, and poets were very angry with World War I and its effects on people's lives. They also wanted to create and practice art in new ways. So they started working together. Their art was called Dadaism.

Dadaism was an art *movement*. A movement is an effort among many people to reach a common goal. The artists in the Dada movement were from Europe and the United States. The movement had many members.

One of their main goals was to get people to think differently about art and beauty. This was very important to the Dadaists. What many people saw as beautiful, the Dadaists saw as boring. So they tried many new things. For example, one Dadaist was named Marcel Duchamp. He created an art display called "Bicycle Wheel." It was simply a bicycle wheel attached to the top of a stool. Many of those who viewed it felt that it did not make sense. But to the Dadaists, that is what made it special.

1. Why did artists, writers, and poets start the Dada movement?

   _____
   _____
   _____
   _____

2. What is a *movement*?

   _____
   _____
   _____

3. An artist paints a picture. The picture has a frame with three sides and no congruent angles. What type of triangle is the frame?

   _____
   _____

Unit 6, Lesson 8   109

Application

YOUR TURN

Read the article below. Then answer the questions.

Dadaism and Surrealism

Dadaism was known for being playful and different. The word *dada* comes from the French word for *hobbyhorse*. The word did not describe the movement or the art. In fact, it made very little sense. According to some sources, however, that is exactly the reason why the artists chose the word—because it made no sense. That is what made the word *dada* beautiful to them.

The art movement of Dadaism started to slow down around 1922. In its place arose a new art movement called Surrealism. Like the Dadaists, the Surrealists wanted to practice art in new and interesting ways. However, Surrealism was different. Something that made little sense was beautiful to a Dadaist. A Surrealist worked to create something that made sense but only if you studied it.

One Surrealist was named Salvador Dali. He painted a picture called *The Persistence of Memory*. It shows clocks that are limp and soft like blankets. On the surface, this does not make sense. However, many people think this picture is Dali's way of saying that our memory is not always correct. People remember the same things in different ways. So the picture makes no sense at first. If you study it, though, you see that it makes perfect sense after all.

1. Where does the word *dada* come from?
   _____
   _____

2. A painter wants to paint a square using only acute angles. Is this possible? Why or why not?
   _____
   _____

3. Which art style do you like most, Dadaism or Surrealism? Why?
   _____
   _____
   _____

Fluency Tip
If you read any words that you do not understand, a dictionary can very helpful.

READ on Your Own

Reading Comprehension

Reading Comprehension Strategy: Visualizing

Artworks, pages 16–18

VOCABULARY

Watch for the words you are learning about.

architecture: the art of designing and building structures

symmetrical: something that shows symmetry or balance

Fluency Tip

As you read and reread, pay attention to punctuation marks that are cues to correct phrasing.

Before You Read

Think about what you read in "Sculpture." Describe a sculpture you have seen recently.

As You Read

Read "Architecture," pages 16–18. 🛑

In each sentence below, underline the descriptive or sensory words. Use the words to form a picture in your mind. Then describe the picture.

They also make sure the buildings are strong and safe.

_____

_____

This cathedral is famous for its many detailed statues and sharp points on its roof.

_____

_____

_____

An architect creating a building overlooking a fast-flowing river may design the building on stilts, high above the raging water.

_____

_____

After You Read

Think of your favorite piece of architecture. Use descriptive or sensory words to help someone visualize it.

_____

_____

Unit 6, Lesson 8

Problem Solving

SOLVE on Your Own

Artworks, page 19

Organize the Information

Use a list like the one below to organize questions and answers about the information you find in the Math Project. Each question in the list will help you as you design your museum.

1. What shapes can I choose from for my rooms?
2. Which shapes have acute angles?
3. Which shapes have obtuse angles?
4. Which shapes have right angles?

Math Project

Use the questions in the list above to answer these questions. Write your answers in the space provided.

1. What was your process for choosing which shapes to use for the rooms?

   _____

   _____

A sketch will help you map out the shape of each room.

2. How can you estimate the total perimeter as you make your design?

   _____

   _____

3. When counting acute and obtuse angles, what patterns do you notice with the polygons?

   _____

After You Solve

How can you change the total perimeter of your museum?

_____

Unit 6, Lesson 8

Put It Together

Connections

Introducing Why Certain Shapes Are Not Polygons

You have learned to identify many different polygons by their angles and their sides. But some shapes are not polygons. Why? There are three important polygon rules.

First, polygons have line segments for sides. The sides cannot be curved. If a side is curved, it is not a polygon. Second, polygons must be closed. You must be able to choose a point on the side and trace the perimeter of the polygon back to the chosen point. If you cannot trace back to the chosen point, the figure is not a polygon. Finally, the sides of the polygon must not cross. If the sides cross, it is not a polygon.

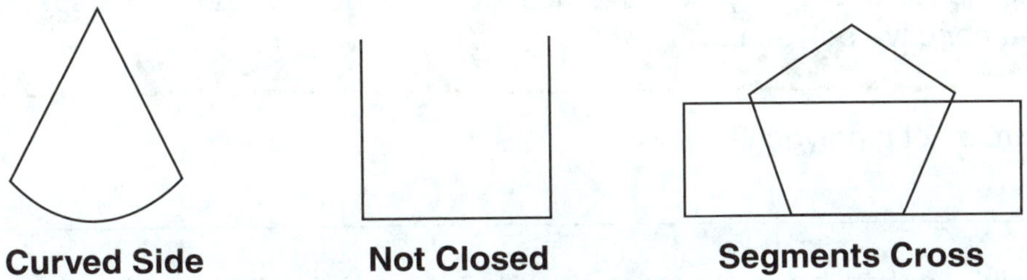

Curved Side   **Not Closed**   **Segments Cross**

A figure is not a polygon if it does not follow all three polygon rules. If a figure breaks one or more of these rules, then it is not a polygon.

Practicing Why Certain Shapes Are Not Polygons

Explain why each of the figures is not a polygon.

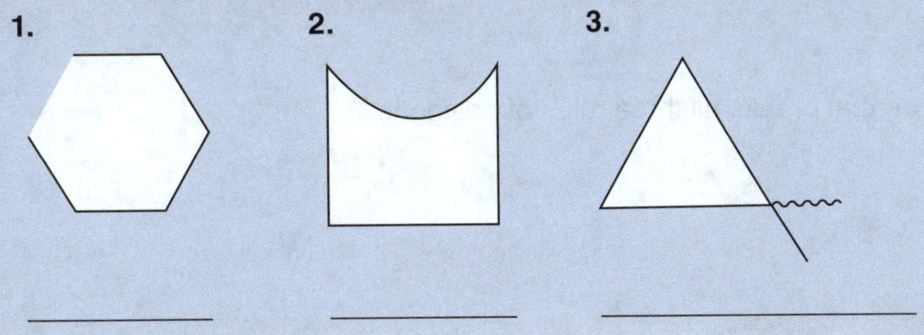

1.

2.

3.

Unit 6, Lesson 9   113

Connections

YOUR TURN

Thinking About Why Certain Shapes Are Not Polygons

Think about the three important polygon rules. Now look at the shape below. It almost looks like a polygon you have seen before, but this figure has one corner pushed inward. Is it a polygon?

Does the shape have any curves? Is the shape closed? Do any of the line segments cross? The figure follows all the rules for polygons, so it must be a polygon. In fact, it is a special type of polygon called a concave polygon.

1. Why is a circle not a polygon?
   _____

2. It is impossible to draw a concave triangle. Why do you think this is so?
   _____
   _____

3. Draw a concave hexagon.

4. Draw a figure that breaks all three rules of polygons.

Tip Once you have identified whether or not a shape is a polygon, take it a step further and try to identify the type of polygon.

Show That You Know

Read the information below. Use what you have learned about the rules of polygons and concave polygons to answer the questions. Use the space provided to show your work.

Amy gets a picture for her bedroom. The picture has many polygons on it, but it also includes some figures that are not polygons. She calls a friend and tries to describe it.

When you describe a shape, start out by saying whether or not it is a polygon, and then move on to other features.

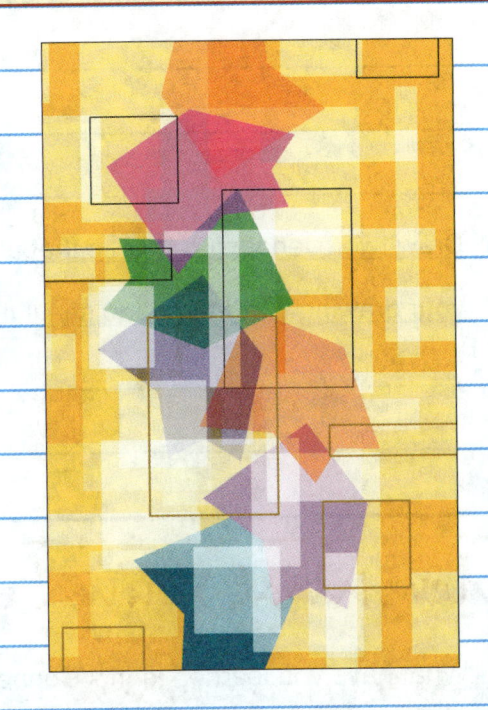

1. What two-dimensional features can Amy use to describe the shapes?

2. If Amy says a figure is not a polygon, what would her friend know about the figure?

3. Do you think it is easier to describe polygons or figures that are not polygons?

4. Can you think of any figures that are not polygons that would be easy to describe?

Unit 6, Lesson 9   115

Connections

Show That You Know (continued)

5. Draw a simple polygon. Then try describing it to a friend. See if they can draw the same polygon from your description.

6. Draw three overlapping polygons. Try to write a description of them. Use angles, lines, and names of polygons in your description.

7. Draw two overlapping figures that are not polygons. Try to describe your drawing to a friend and see if they can draw what you describe.

Review What You've Learned

8. What have you learned in this Connections lesson about identifying figures that are not polygons?

9. What have you learned in this Connections lesson that you did not already know?

10. How will this lesson help you identify unusual shapes?

Review and Practice

Skills Review

Polygons
Closed figures with at least three sides, including triangles, quadrilaterals, pentagons and others, are polygons.

The perimeter of a polygon is the sum of the lengths of the sides of the polygon.

Regular polygons
A regular polygon has congruent sides.

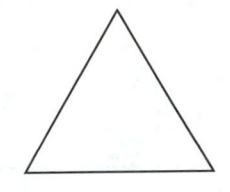

Acute and obtuse angles
Angles that measure between 0° and 90° are acute angles. A 35° angle is acute.

Angles that measure between 90° and 180° are obtuse angles. A 115° angle is obtuse.

Right angles and straight angles
A 90° angle is a right angle.

A 180° angle is a straight angle. This type of angle looks like a straight line.

Classifying triangles
Equilateral triangles have three congruent sides and angles.

Isosceles triangles have at least two congruent sides.

Scalene triangles have no congruent sides.

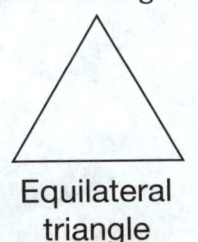

Equilateral triangle   Isosceles triangle   Scalene triangle

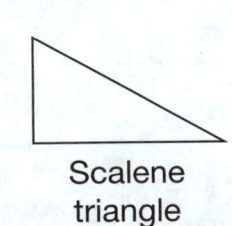

Classifying quadrilaterals
Parallelograms have two pairs of opposite sides that are parallel. A rectangle is a parallelogram with all right angles. A rhombus is a parallelogram that has four congruent sides. A square is a rhombus and a rectangle. It has all right angles and four congruent sides.

Parallelogram   Square   Rectangle

Strategy Review

- Several common objects are shaped like polygons, such as bricks (rectangle), stop signs (octagon), and roofs (triangle). These objects can be used to model polygons.
- Use pictures and make a table listing descriptions to help you remember the different types of polygons.
- Use a clock to estimate angles. The angle formed by the clock hands at 3 o'clock is 90°, at 6 o'clock its 180°, and at 12 o'clock the angle is 0°.
- A 45° angle and its multiples can be used as a reference for comparing angles.

Unit 6, Lesson 10

Review and Practice

Skills and Strategies Practice

Complete the exercises below.

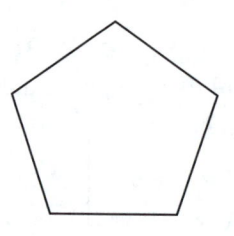

1. Is this figure a regular polygon? Why?

    _____

2. Estimate the measure of an angle formed by the hands of a clock at 12:20 P.M.

    _____

3. What is the perimeter of a regular quadrilateral with a side that is 4 ft long?

    _____

4. A 27° angle is a(n) _____ angle. Draw the angle below.

5. What is the measure of the angles of a rectangle?

    _____

6. What do an equilateral triangle, a square, and a rhombus have in common?

    _____

Test-Taking tip: To study for a test on polygons, write the name of each type of polygon you have learned about in this unit on one side of an index card. On the other side, write the definition of the type of polygon, followed by a picture of an example. Use the cards to quiz a partner on the different polygons. You can show your partner the side with the name of the polygon or the side with the example and definition. Your partner must say back the definition or the type of polygon.

Mid-Unit Review

Circle the letter of the correct answer.

1. Which of these shapes is a regular polygon?

   A. a triangle with a 2-in side, a 3-in. side, and a 3-in. side
   B. a triangle with a 5-ft side and a 4.5-ft side
   C. a quadrilateral with two 12-ft sides and a 23-ft side
   D. a square with four 6-in. sides

2. What type of polygon has four sides?

   A. hexagon   C. triangle
   B. quadrilateral   D. pentagon

3. Which group shows only acute angles?

   A. 77°, 27°, 119°, 97°   C. 57°, 27°, 89°, 87°
   B. 77°, 26°, 32°, 117°   D. 67°, 27°, 135°, 117°

4. What is the perimeter of a pentagon with sides that measure: 3 yd, 4 yd, 1 yd, 6 yd, and 13 yd?

   A. 27 yd   B. 26 yd   C. 14 yd   D. 24 yd

5. A square is also a(n) _____.

   A. rhombus   C. hexagon
   B. irregular polygon   D. pentagon

6. Which measurement shows an acute angle?

   A. 12°   B. 92°   C. 180°   D. 119°

7. What is the perimeter of an equilateral triangle with 9-ft sides?

   A. 18 ft   B. 27 ft   C. 36 ft   D. 9 ft

8. A shape has five sides. This shape is a(n) _____.

   A. octagon   C. hexagon
   B. square   D. pentagon

9. A quadrilateral with no right angles but two pairs of parallel sides is a _____.

   A. square   C. parallelogram
   B. rectangle   D. triangle

10. What is the perimeter of a square with a side that measures 22 feet?

    A. 22 ft   B. 44 ft   C. 66 ft   D. 88 ft

11. Which group shows only obtuse angles?

    A. 113°, 22°, 88°, 97°
    B. 117°, 26°, 92°, 115°
    C. 57°, 7°, 93°, 87°
    D. 113°, 99°, 135°, 117°

12. An isosceles triangle has a 6-in. side and a 14-in. side. What could be the length of the third side?

    A. 6 in.   B. 8 in.   C. 10 in.   D. 26 in.

13. Which angle looks like a straight line?

    A. acute angle   C. obtuse angle
    B. 180° angle   D. right angle

Unit 6, Lesson 10

Review and Practice

Mid-Unit Review

14. What is the perimeter of a rectangle with two 2-in. sides and two 36-in. sides?

    A. 76 in.   B. 40 in.   C. 72 in.   D. 38 in.

15. A square has sides that are 6 ft long. What is the perimeter?

    A. 24 ft   B. 20 ft   C. 16 ft   D. 40 ft

16. What kind of triangle has all equal sides?

    A. equilateral   C. isosceles
    B. scalene   D. obtuse

17. An octagon is a polygon with how many sides?

    A. 4   B. 3   C. 6   D. 8

18. Which set could show the side measurements of a scalene triangle?

    A. 9 in., 5 in., 5 in.   C. 4 in., 9 in., 6 in.
    B. 6 in., 6 in., 6 in.   D. 9 in., 9 in., 1 in.

19. Which set could show the angle measurements of an equilateral triangle?

    A. 90°, 45°, 45°   C. 24°, 90°, 66°
    B. 60°, 60°, 60°   D. 90°, 90°, 0°

20. A polygon has sides of the following lengths: 1 in., 1 in., 15 in., 1 in., and 3 in. What is the perimeter?

    A. 22 in.   B. 21 in.   C. 18 in.   D. 17 in.

21. A polygon has three sides measuring 17 in., 16 in., and 17 in. What type of polygon is it?

    A. regular polygon
    B. isosceles triangle
    C. equilateral triangle
    D. parallelogram

22. An angle that measures 145° is what type of angle?

    A. straight   C. regular
    B. obtuse   D. acute

23. What is the measurement of a right angle?

    A. 0°   B. 180°   C. 90°   D. 100°

24. Which shape is a regular polygon with four sides?

    A. trapezoid   C. scalene triangle
    B. square   D. rectangle

25. A hexagon in which all sides are 88 cm long is what type of polygon?

    A. similar   C. parallel
    B. straight   D. regular

Learn the Skill

Decomposing, Combining, and Transforming Polygons

Learn the SKILL

Betty wants to create a puzzle of a rectangle. She wants all the puzzle pieces to be triangles. How can she make a rectangle from triangles?

VOCABULARY
Watch for the words you are learning about.

combined shapes: shapes that are made of two or more polygons

decompose: to break apart a shape into other shapes

rotation: a transformation that turns a figure about a fixed center point

transformation: a change in the position, shape, or size of a figure

translation: a transformation that slides each point of a figure the same distance and in the same direction

SKILL	EXAMPLE	WRITE AN EXAMPLE
A polygon can be **decomposed**, or broken down into other shapes. For example, polygons can be decomposed into rectangles, squares, and/or triangles.	How can you decompose a rectangle into triangles? 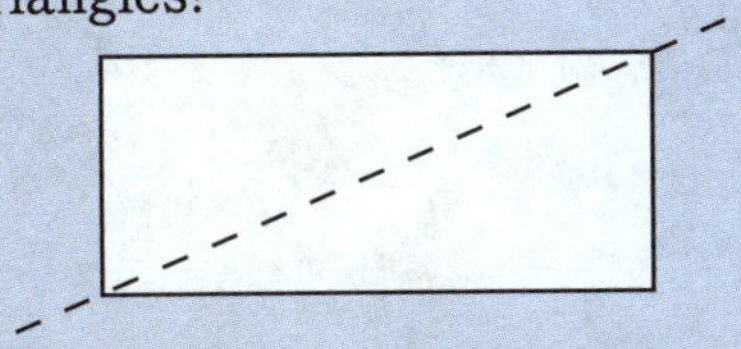 Cut the rectangle in half from one corner to the opposite corner.	How can you decompose a rectangle into a rectangle or square and two triangles? _____
Polygons can be made from **combined shapes.** For example two triangles can be combined to form a parallelogram.	How many triangles are combined to form a pentagon? 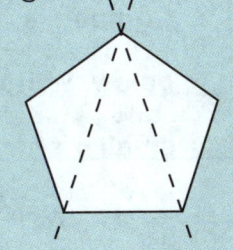 Three triangles are combined.	How many triangles can be combined to form a square? _____
Polygons can also show **transformations.** In a **translation,** the polygon changes location. In a **rotation,** the polygon is turned about a fixed point.	What transformation is shown? 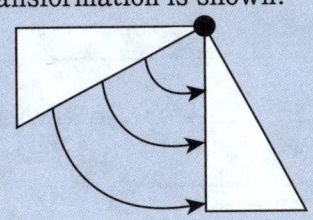 This transformation is a rotation.	A whole triangle is moved from right to left. It is not turned. What transformation has taken place? _____

Unit 6, Lesson 11   121

Learn the Skill

YOUR TURN

Choose the Right Word

> combined   decompose
> rotation   translation

Fill in each blank with the correct word or phrase from the box.

1. Two triangles can be _____ to form a rectangle.

2. A _____ is a transformation where you change the location of a polygon.

3. When you _____ a polygon, you break it into other shapes, such as rectangles and triangles.

4. A triangle is turned about a central point during a _____.

Yes or No?

Answer these questions and be ready to explain your answers.

5. Can a rectangle ever be decomposed into squares? _____

6. If a triangle is turned, is it being translated? _____

7. Can a triangle be decomposed into only rectangles? _____

8. Is it possible that a polygon can be decomposed into both triangles and rectangles? _____

Show That You Know

Decompose the polygons below into smaller shapes. Write the name and number of the smaller shapes you use.

9. triangle

10. pentagon

11. rectangle

Combine smaller shapes to form the polygons below. Write the name and number of the smaller shapes you use.

12. square

13. trapezoid

14. parallelogram

SOLVE on Your Own

Skills Practice

Quite often, there is more than one way to decompose or combine shapes.

Decompose the shapes below. Write the name and number of the shapes you use.

1. rectangle _____

2. parallelogram _____

3. equilateral triangle _____

4. _____

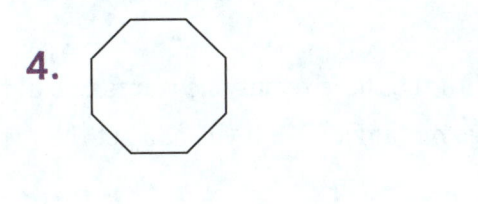

5. _____

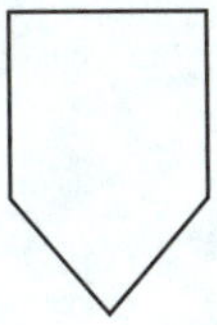

Combine the shapes below to make a larger polygon. Write the type of polygon you make.

6. two triangles _____

7. one rectangle and two triangles _____

8. four triangles _____

9. one trapezoid and two triangles _____

10. one rectangle and one triangle _____

Name the transformation shown.

11. _____

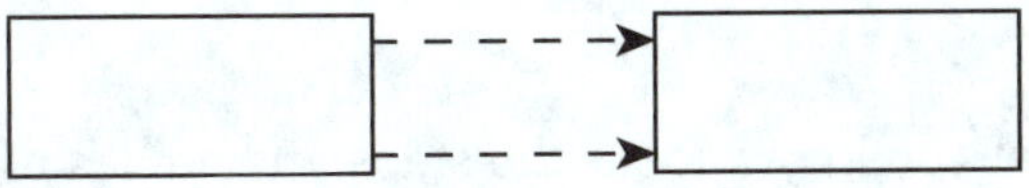

12. _____

Unit 6, Lesson 11   123

Choose a Strategy

Decomposing, Combining, and Transforming Polygons

Strategies

Draw a Picture or Use a Model;
Guess, Check and Revise

Step 1: Read A builder is designing a new addition to her home. She wants the addition to have a large square bedroom, a small square bathroom, and a rectangular hall connecting them. She wants the entire addition to be shaped like a rectangle. Can she design the rooms so, when connected, they form a large rectangle?

STRATEGY	SOLUTION
Draw a Picture or Use a Model You can use manipulatives such as pattern blocks to decompose and combine shapes. If you do not have pattern blocks, you can draw shapes on paper, cut them out, and see how the pieces fit together.	**Step 2: Plan** Draw the shapes of the rooms on paper. Cut them out. Combine them to see if they can form a large rectangle. **Step 3: Solve** Start [bedroom, bathroom, hall] Finish [bedroom, hall, bathroom] Yes, she can form a large rectangle with the three rooms she wants to build. **Step 4: Check** Decompose a large rectangle. See if you can get the same shapes you started with.
Guess, Check, and Revise Sometimes, you may think you know how the shapes can be combined without using manipulatives. In that case, drawing your guess and checking it can be faster.	**Step 2: Plan** Draw how you think she can arrange her rooms into a large rectangle. Revise your drawing if you need to. **Step 3: Solve** No [bedroom, hall, bathroom] Yes [bedroom, hall, bathroom] **Step 4: Check** Use what you know about the sides and angles of polygons to see if the shape you have is truly a rectangle. Are opposite sides parallel? Is each angle a right angle?

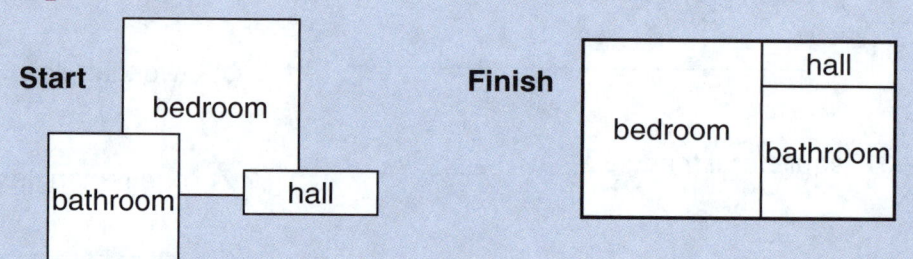

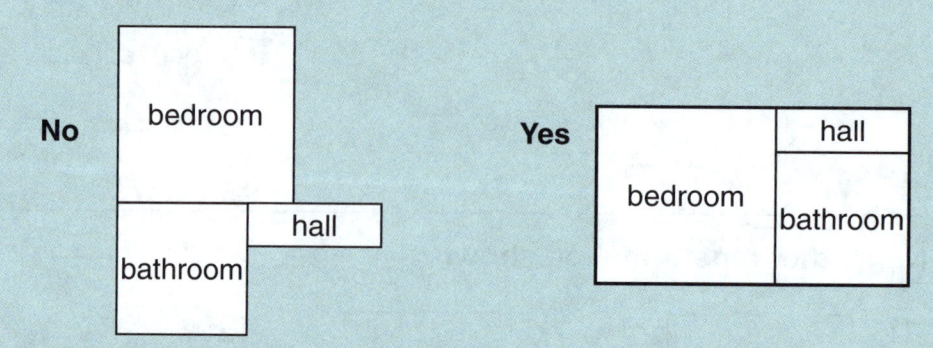

YOUR TURN

Choose the Right Word

> combined shapes
> decompose   transformation

Fill in each blank with the correct word or phrase from the box.

1. You can _____ a large polygon into smaller polygons.

2. A translation is an example of a _____.

3. Polygons formed from two or more smaller shapes are _____.

Choose a Strategy

Yes or No?

Answer these questions and be ready to explain your answers.

4. Is the perimeter of a large polygon equal to the perimeters of its smaller, combined shapes? _____

5. Are all combined shapes regular polygons? _____

6. Are there any polygons you cannot decompose? _____

7. Are transformations useful when combining shapes? _____

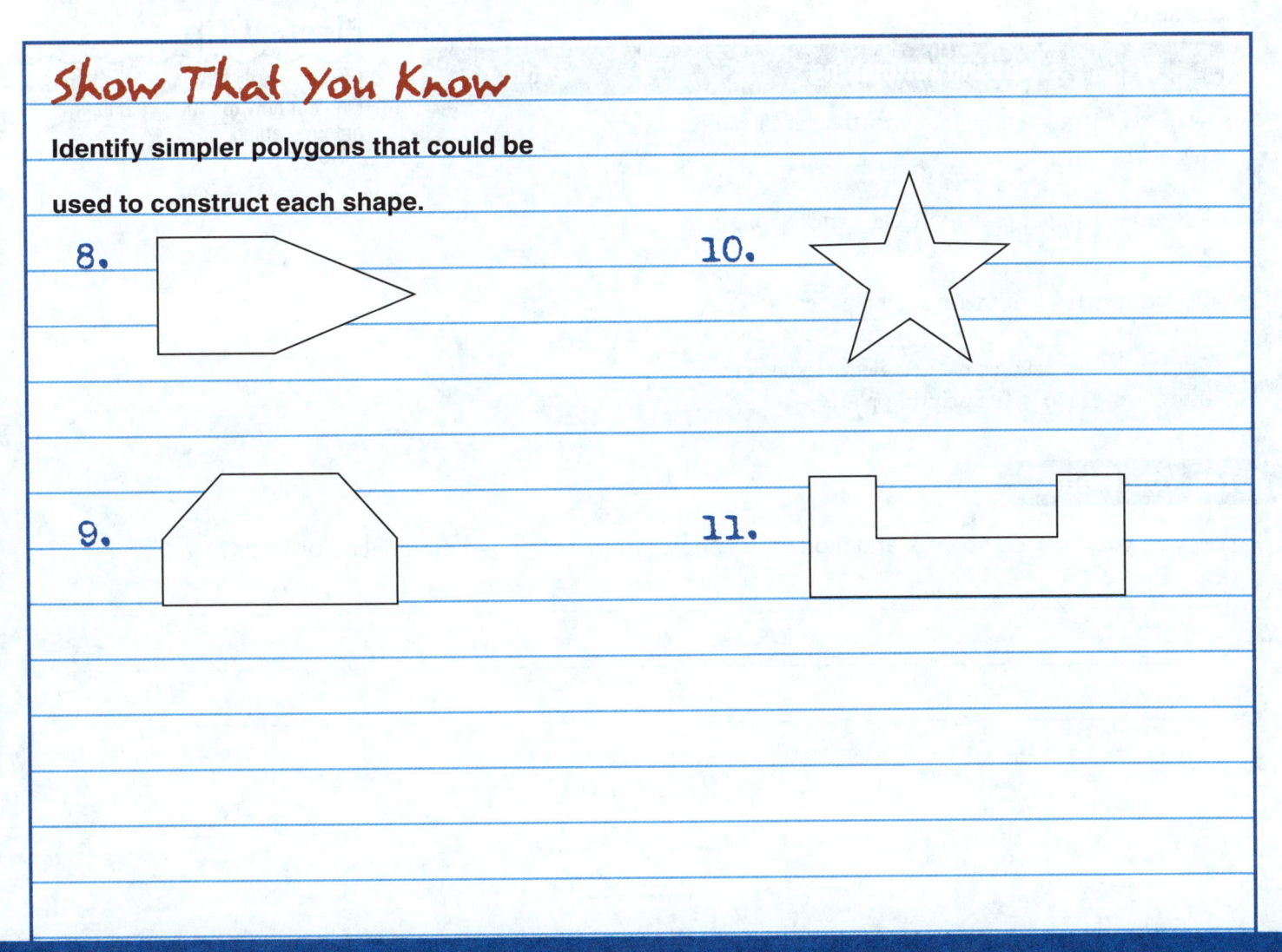

Show That You Know

Identify simpler polygons that could be used to construct each shape.

8.

9.

10.

11.

Unit 6, Lesson 12   125

Reading Comprehension

READ on Your Own

Reading Comprehension Strategy: Visualizing

Artworks, pages 20–21

VOCABULARY

Watch for the words you are learning about.

lithography: a method of printing from a flat surface that has been prepared so that only the area meant to print will take ink

printing plate: a metal plate with an image used for printing pictures

registration: a careful process of using many printing plates to created a single color picture

relief printing: a printmaking process in which a printing surface is cut into the shape of an image

Fluency Tip

Identify words that you do not know. Find out how to pronounce them before reading.

Before You Read

Think about what you read in "Sculpture." What steps do you think are involved in making sculptures?

As You Read

Read "Printmaking," pages 20–21. STOP

Then read the steps of printmaking listed in the chart below. In the second column, write the numbers 1 to 4 to show the correct order of the steps.

Steps in Printmaking	Order
Wipe off extra paint so that only the cut lines hold the color.	
Use a roller to put paint onto the printing plate.	
Use a press to print the image on paper.	
Cut the mirror images of the objects to be printed into the surface of the printing plate.	

After You Read

How do you think computers and modern technology have changed the printing process?

_____
_____
_____

Problem Solving

SOLVE on Your Own

Artworks, page 12

Organize the Information

Read You Do the Math in the magazine. Then complete the chart below to keep track of each step of the process.

Step 1	Step 2	Step 3	Step 4
Break a rectangle into a right triangle, a square, a parallelogram, and two other polygons.			

You Do the Math

Use the information in the chart above to answer these questions. Write your answers in the space provided.

> Listing possible combinations of shapes may help you answer the magazine questions.

1. What five polygons did you use?

   _____

2. What can you do to adjust the perimeter of one of your complex polygons?

   _____
   _____
   _____
   _____

After You Solve

What will happen to each of the puzzle images when you print them onto T-shirts?

_____
_____

Unit 6, Lesson 12

Learn the Skill

Building, Drawing, and Analyzing Two-Dimensional Shapes

VOCABULARY
Watch for the words you are learning about.

acute triangle: a triangle with all angles measuring less than 90°

complementary angles: two angles for which the sum of their measures is 90°

obtuse triangle: a triangle with one obtuse angle

right triangle: a triangle with one angle measuring 90°

supplementary angles: two angles for which the sum of their measures is 180°

Learn the SKILL

Cody is learning about drawing triangles and combining angles. He wants to make a 45° angle. He also wants to figure out if he can combine any three lines to make a triangle. How can he do this?

SKILL	EXAMPLE	WRITE AN EXAMPLE
A triangle that has all acute angles is called an **acute triangle.** A triangle with one right angle is called a **right triangle.** A triangle with one obtuse angle is called an **obtuse triangle.**	State if the triangle is an acute triangle, a right triangle, or an obtuse triangle. 35° 55° This is a right triangle.	Draw a triangle. Label it as a right, acute, or obtuse triangle.
Pairs of angles with measures that add to 90° are called **complementary angles.** Pairs of angles with measures that add to 180° are called **supplementary angles.**	Which pair of angles is complementary? 40°/50° 50°/50° The two angles on the left are complementary because the sum of their measures is 90°.	Draw two supplementary angles. Label their measurements.
In a triangle, the sum of any two sides is greater than the third side.	Can you draw a triangle with side lengths of 10 in., 12 in., and 24 in.? No, because 10 in. + 12 in. < 24 in.	Can you draw a triangle with side lengths of $\frac{1}{2}$ in., $1\frac{1}{2}$ in., and 1 in.?

Unit 6, Lesson 13

YOUR TURN

Choose the Right Word

> complementary   obtuse
> straight angle   supplementary

Fill in each blank with the correct word or phrase from the box.

1. A straight line is also considered a(n) _____.

2. Two angles whose measures add to 90° are _____.

3. A(n) _____ angle is greater than 90°.

4. An obtuse angle has an acute _____ angle.

Yes or No?

Answer these questions and be ready to explain your answers.

5. If a triangle has a right angle, could it also have an obtuse angle? _____

6. Can you build a straight angle using an angle that is 67°? _____

7. Is 99° a right angle? _____

8. Can you draw a triangle with side lengths of 5 inches, 12 inches, and 13 inches? _____

Show That You Know

Write your answers to the questions below.

9. What angle is supplementary to 165°?

10. What angle is complementary to 45°?

11. If two sides of a triangle are 3 cm and 10 cm, how long might the third side be?

12. What is another name for this triangle?

    (triangle with angles 100°, 40°, 40°)

13. What angle can you add to 60° to form a straight angle?

14. What angle can you add to 140° to form a straight angle?

Unit 6, Lesson 13   129

Learn the Skill

SOLVE on Your Own

Skills Practice

Use a protractor to help you find the angles you need.

Find the complementary angle.

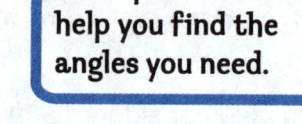

1. 65° _____

2. 89° _____

3. 27° _____

Identify these triangles.

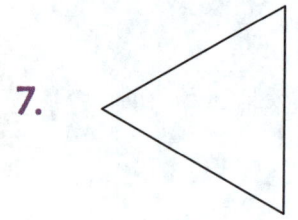

7. _____
   _____

8. _____
   _____

Draw a triangle with the given side lengths on another sheet of paper. Write "possible" or "not possible" on the lines below.

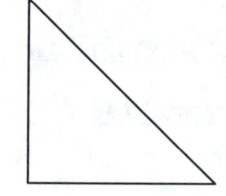

4. 3 cm, 4 cm, 5 cm _____

5. 10 cm, 12 cm, 1 cm _____

6. 1 in., 4 in., 6 in. _____

Find the supplementary angle.

9. 60° _____

10. 145° _____

11. 10° _____

130   Unit 6, Lesson 13

Choose a Strategy

Building, Drawing, and Analyzing Two-Dimensional Shapes

Strategy
Draw a Picture or Use a Model

Step 1: Read Callie wants to make a patchwork quilt out of equal-sized triangles. The angle measurements of these triangles are 30°, 70°, and 80°. How can she put these triangles together to get a quilt with at least two straight sides?

STRATEGY	SOLUTION
Draw a Picture or Use a Model Paper models of shapes can help you think through and visualize the possibilities. Paper shapes can also be rotated or translated easily.	**Step 2: Plan** Make paper models of the triangles. Then combine the shapes in different ways to see if a quilt with straight edges is possible. **Step 3: Solve** Use a protractor and scissors to make the paper triangles that match the angle measurements of the quilt triangles. Rotate and combine the triangles as needed until you find a way to make a straight edge. **Step 4: Check** Add the angles along one edge to see if they form a 180° angle. A 180° angle is a straight angle or a straight line. 70 + 30 + 80 = 180

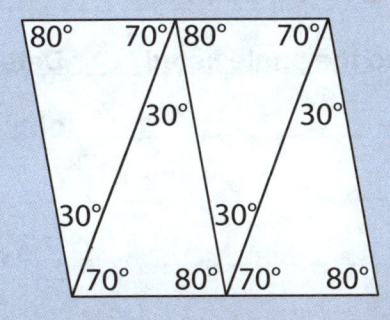

Unit 6, Lesson 14 131

Choose a Strategy

YOUR TURN

Choose the Right Word

acute triangle   right triangle   straight angle

Fill in each blank with the correct word or phrase from the box.

1. A three-sided polygon in which all the angles are less than 90° is a(n) _____.

2. A(n) _____ has only one angle with a measure of 90°.

3. An angle with a measure of 180° is a(n) _____.

Yes or No?

Answer these questions and be ready to explain your answers.

4. Can a right triangle be divided into two acute triangles? _____

5. Can a triangle ever have two 90° angles? _____

6. Can any two triangles be combined to form a square? _____

7. Can a triangle be a right triangle and have an obtuse angle? _____

Show That You Know

Add two more angles to the angle listed to form a straight angle.

8. 40°.

9. 45°

10. 99°

11. 70°

12. 110°

Determine if each triangle is an acute triangle, an obtuse triangle, or a right triangle.

13. a triangle with 34°, 66°, and 80° angles

14. a triangle with 45°, 40°, and 95° angles

15. a triangle with 42°, 48°, and 90° angles

132   Unit 6, Lesson 14

READ on Your Own

Reading Comprehension Strategy: Visualizing

Artworks, pages 23–24

Before You Read

Think about what you learned in "Printmaking." How do you think the invention of the printing press affected the craft of copying books by hand?

As You Read

Read "Crafts," pages 23–24. 🛑

Then create a picture in your mind of the events described in "Weaving" on page 23. Complete the chart below by numbering the four events in the order in which they likely occurred.

Event	Order
In Colonial times, sheep were sheared so their wool could be woven into cloth.	
Weaving began in prehistoric days.	
The loom was brought to the United States in the early 1820s.	
In the 1600s, weaving was the main craft of the Navajo tribe of American Indians.	

After You Read

Weaving is not just used to make clothes. What other useful products might be made by weaving?

_____

_____

VOCABULARY

Watch for the words you are learning about.

digital: involving computer or electronic technology

fibers: strands of any thin, thread-like material

loom: a frame or machine used to make cloth

weaving: an art in which strands of fiber are laced together to make cloth

Fluency Tip

Everyone reads at a different pace. Practice until you can read at a pace that is comfortable for you.

Problem Solving

SOLVE on Your Own

Artworks, *page 25*

Organize the Information

Read You Do the Math in the magazine. Then complete the following table for the polygons listed.

Polygons	Number of Acute Angles	Number of Right Angles	Number of Obtuse Angles
acute triangle	3	0	0
obtuse triangle			
right triangle			
parallelogram			
trapezoid			
square or rectangle			

You Do the Math

Use the information in the table above to answer these questions. Write your answers in the space provided.

Drawing the shapes you might want to use may help you answer the magazine questions.

1. Look at the column for the Number of Acute Angles in the table above. What does this column tell you about the number of acute triangles your plan should include?

   _____
   _____
   _____

2. Which polygons can you use to follow all of the rules?

   _____
   _____

After You Solve

Do the angles provided in the rules limit the size of the shapes?

_____

134   Unit 6, Lesson 14

Solve It!

Application

The Four-Step Problem-Solving Plan

Step 1: Read	Step 2: Plan	Step 3: Solve	Step 4: Check
Make sure you understand what the problem is asking.	Decide how you will solve the problem.	Solve the problem using your plan.	Check to make sure your answer is correct.

Read the article below. Then answer the questions.

Artists and Computers

We use computers for many things. We use them to set up appointments, communicate, and buy everything from music to food. Artists can even use a computer to create art. They can edit videos, design sculpture, change photographs, and make prints.

The idea behind computer art, or digital art, was to move beyond making art that could only be shown on the walls of museums and galleries. Artists wanted to break away from the old ways of painting or drawing. The history of digital art is also a part of the history of computer technology. As technology grew, it gave artists new ways to express themselves.

One of the earliest forms of digital art was made in 1958 when John Whitney Sr. used an analog computer for animation. The first computer art competition followed in 1963. The growing world of technology in art led to the world's first solo exhibition of computer art in 1971. From there, artists were able to display their art and learn from each other.

1. What are some ways artists use computers?

   _____
   _____
   _____
   _____

2. An artist displayed his drawings on a rectangular wall measuring 20 feet high by 40 feet wide. After a few months, he moved his drawings to two smaller walls with the same total area. What could be the dimensions of the two walls if they were equal in size? What shape would they be?

   _____
   _____
   _____
   _____
   _____
   _____

Unit 6, Lesson 15

Application

YOUR TURN

Read the article below. Then answer the questions.

Digital Art in Homes and Business

As computers became more and more powerful, more people were able to create digital art. Entire computer systems were created for the purpose of making digital art and graphics. These systems were first available in the early 1980s. Businesses began using computers to create digital art in advertising. Television and news networks used the new technology to animate program titles, logos, and weather maps.

Many art programs for using at home followed. With each passing year, programs improved and could do more and more. By 1989, programs were available for using at home that could digitally change photographs.

The Internet allowed people to share the digital art they created. As more and more people created digital art, it became accepted as serious art. This led to Wolfgang Lieser's creation in 1998 of the Digital Art Museum. This museum serves as an online museum that shows the work of the world's leading digital artists.

Fluency Tip

If you find yourself reading so quickly that you do not understand what you are reading, slow down.

1. What might be some advantages to drawing a picture on a computer instead of drawing a picture on paper?

   _____
   _____

2. What might be some advantages to drawing a picture on paper instead of drawing a picture on a computer?

   _____
   _____
   _____

3. An artist made a drawing that measures 3 inches by 2 inches. She then scanned the drawing into her computer and used a program to triple the drawing's length and width. What are the dimensions of the computer drawing?

   _____

READ on Your Own

Reading Comprehension Strategy: Visualizing

Artworks, pages 26–28

VOCABULARY
Watch for the words you are learning about.

pixels: small elements that make up an image

Fluency Tip
As you read and reread, pay attention to punctuation marks that are clues to correct phrasing.

Before You Read

Think about what you read in "Crafts." How has technology changed the way crafts are made?

As You Read

Read "Digital Art," pages 26–28. STOP

Then create a picture in your mind of the sequence of events in the history of motion pictures. Complete the chart below by numbering the events in the order in which they likely occurred.

Events	Order
In the late 1920s, sound was added to films.	
Improvements in technology allowed for improved digital photography.	
Video tape was developed for television.	
The first films were silent films.	

After You Read

What is one new piece of information you learned from this article?

_____

_____

_____

Unit 6, Lesson 15   137

Problem Solving

SOLVE on Your Own

Artworks, page 29

Organize the Information

Use a list like the one below to organize the information you find in the Math Project in the magazine.

Polygon	Possible Robot Part
triangle	
square	middle of body
rectangle	
hexagon	
octagon	

Math Project

Use the information in the table above to answer these questions. Write your answers in the space provided.

1. Look at the shape of your robot. Is it possible to cover the entire shape of the robot with other polygons?

   _____
   _____

2. What makes rotations difficult with complex polygons?

   _____
   _____

You may find more than one place to use a particular shape in your robot.

After You Solve

How could a computer make it easier to make a flip book?

_____
_____
_____

138   Unit 6, Lesson 15

Congruence and Symmetry

Learn the SKILL

VOCABULARY

Watch for the words you are learning about.

line of symmetry: a line that divides a figure into mirror images

symmetry: a figure has symmetry if it can be folded along a line so both parts match exactly

Joe is studying origami, the Japanese art of paper folding, in his social studies class. He wants to fold a rectangular piece of paper into an origami flower. For the first step, Joe needs to fold the paper in half, diagonally. For the second step, he must unfold the rectangle. The fold line in the paper should reveal two triangles. Are these triangles congruent?

SKILL	EXAMPLE	WRITE AN EXAMPLE
If two figures have exactly the same size and shape, they are congruent. The parts that are exactly equal are congruent parts.	Why are these figures congruent? The shapes have the same size and shape.	Draw two congruent figures.
A rectangle can be decomposed with a diagonal line to form two congruent triangles. The angles and sides are congruent parts, which are exactly equal.	Are Joe's two triangles congruent? Yes. The sides of the rectangle are equal and each make up one side of the triangle. The third line is shared by both triangles.	How can you create two congruent triangles from a square? Draw your answer.
A figure has **symmetry** if it can be folded so both halves match exactly. A **line of symmetry** shows how a shape can be folded to show two matching sides. The diagonal of a rectangle is *not* a line of symmetry, since the two sides do not match.	Where would you draw a line of symmetry on a rectangle? This rectangle shows two lines of symmetry. You can fold it either way to make to halves that match exactly.	Draw a line of symmetry on this square.

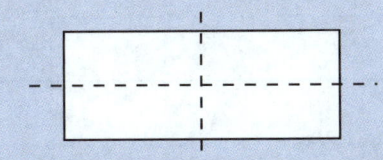

Unit 6, Lesson 16

Learn the Skill

YOUR TURN

Choose the Right Word

> congruent   line of symmetry   symmetry

Fill in each blank with the correct word or phrase from the box.

1. A figure has _____ if it can be folded along a line so both parts match exactly.

2. The _____ divides a figure into exact halves.

3. Figures that have the same size and shape are _____.

Yes or No?

Answer these questions and be ready to explain your answers.

4. Is the diagonal line that forms two triangles in a square a line of symmetry? _____

5. Is the diagonal line that forms two triangles in a rectangle a line of symmetry? _____

6. Are all squares congruent? _____

7. Are the two shapes formed by a line of symmetry congruent? _____

Show That You Know

Explain why these figures are congruent.

8.

Draw a line of symmetry on these two figures.

9.

Because they can lay on top of each other and have no diffrence

10.

140   Unit 6, Lesson 16

SOLVE on Your Own

Skills Practice

Okay, now you know all about congruence and symmetry. Show it by solving these problems.

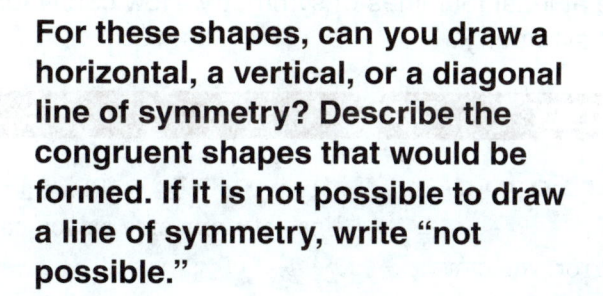

For each set of figures, write if they are congruent or not congruent.

1. _congruent_

2. _Not_

3. _No_

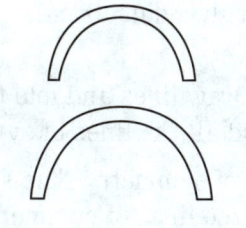

4. _Yes_

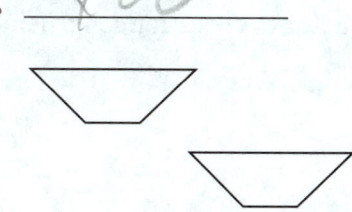

For these shapes, can you draw a horizontal, a vertical, or a diagonal line of symmetry? Describe the congruent shapes that would be formed. If it is not possible to draw a line of symmetry, write "not possible."

5. a square _____

6. a rectangle _____

7. a right triangle _____

8. a diamond _____

9. a parallelogram with no right angles
_____

10. a circle _____

Unit 6, Lesson 16   141

Choose a Strategy

Congruence and Symmetry

Strategies

Try a Simpler Form of the Problem, Draw a Picture or Use a Model

Step 1: Read Nadia is making a pattern to use as a backdrop for a classroom bulletin board. She can use regular pentagons, isosceles triangles, or squares in her pattern. She only wants to use shapes that have at least four lines of symmetry. How can Nadia check for lines of symmetry?

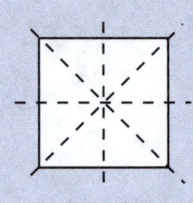

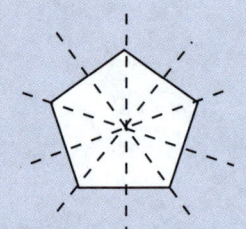

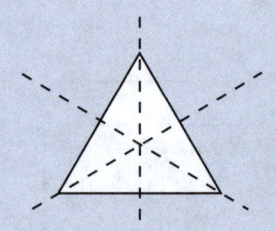

STRATEGY	SOLUTION
Try a Simpler Form of the Problem If you have a mirror, you can place it lengthwise across the shape, as if you are "cutting" with it. The mirror should show the other half of the shape if the shape is symmetrical.	**Step 2: Plan** Place a mirror on each shape and check for as many lines of symmetry as you can. **Step 3: Solve** The pentagon has five lines of symmetry. The square has four lines of symmetry. The triangle has three lines of symmetry. Nadia can use pentagons and squares in her pattern. **Step 4: Check** Use a ruler or a protractor to check of the sides and angles are congruent. If so, than the shape is truly symmetrical.
Draw a Picture or Use a Model If a mirror is not available, you can draw a picture of each shape. You can then fold the picture in half to check for symmetry.	**Step 2: Plan** Draw each shape on paper. Draw lines and fold to check for symmetry. Keep looking until you have found all the lines of symmetry. **Step 3: Solve** The pentagon has five lines of symmetry. The square has four lines of symmetry. The triangle has three lines of symmetry. Nadia can use pentagons and squares. **Step 4: Check** Use a ruler or a protractor to check for congruent sides and angles.

YOUR TURN

Choose a Strategy

Choose the Right Word

congruent   line of symmetry   symmetry

Fill in each blank with the correct word or phrase from the box.

1. A figure has _____ if both halves are folded and match exactly.
2. A _____ will divide a shape into two congruent halves.
3. If two shapes are the mirror image of each other, they are _____.

Yes or No?

Answer these questions and be ready to explain your answers.

4. Does a square only have one line of symmetry? _____
5. Will the mirror image of any shape also be congruent to that shape? _____
6. Will the diameter of a circle also be a line of symmetry for that circle? _____
7. If a line cuts a shape in half, will both halves of the shape always be congruent? _____

Show That You Know

Draw the following shapes with all their lines of symmetry.

8. square

10. a regular octagon

9. equilateral triangle

11. a five-pointed star

Unit 6, Lesson 17

Reading Comprehension

READ on Your Own

Reading Comprehension Strategy: Visualizing

Artworks, pages 30–31

Before You Read

Think about what you read in "Digital Art." How are film photography and digital photography alike and different?

As You Read

Read "Egyptian Art," pages 30–31. 🛑

Then list the descriptive phrases from the second paragraph on page 30 in the left column of the chart below. Draw a picture in the right column of a mental image you formed as you read the paragraph.

Descriptive Phrases	My Mental Image
_____	
_____	
_____	
_____	
_____	
_____	
_____	

VOCABULARY

Watch for the words you are learning about.

frontalism: an Egyptian style of art in which people are shown from the front, but their faces and legs are turned to the side

hieroglyphics: a system of writing made up of pictures and symbols

Fluency Tip

If you find yourself reading so quickly that you are missing the meaning, slow down.

After You Read

The Egyptians used colors to represent their ideas about the world. How do different colors affect the way you feel about something?

_____
_____

Problem Solving

SOLVE on Your Own

Artworks, *page 32*

Organize the Information

Read You Do the Math in the magazine. Then complete the table below to organize information about the different ways to transform a polygon.

Polygon	Translations	Rotations

You Do the Math

Use the information in the table above to answer these questions. Write your answers in the space provided.

1. When creating your code, which polygon was the easiest to use. Why?

   _____
   _____

2. Which polygon was the hardest to use? Why?

   _____
   _____

Drawing a picture may help you answer the magazine questions.

After You Solve

Which letters in our own alphabet have lines of symmetry? What words could you construct that would be perfectly symmetrical?

_____
_____

Unit 6, Lesson 17   145

Application

Solve It!

The Four-Step Problem-Solving Plan

Step 1: Read	Step 2: Plan	Step 3: Solve	Step 4: Check
Make sure you understand what the problem is asking.	Decide how you will solve the problem.	Solve the problem using your plan.	Check to make sure your answer is correct.

Read the article below. Then answer the questions.

Quilting

Quilting's history can be traced back to ancient times. An examination of ancient artwork shows that quilting was used as clothing. During the Middle Ages, people of the Middle East were already making quilts. In fact, they used quilted clothing as part of their soldiers' armor. Europeans may have adapted this tradition when they came into contact with Middle Eastern cultures.

Quilting as clothing changed over time. In 17th-century France, people wore petticoats and outer clothing made from quilted material. At the same time, the French also used quilting as part of their bed coverings.

Quilts were also used to cover the beds in England. It was common for both the rich and the poor. However, the quilts of the rich were stuffed with wool or cotton while the poor had to use old blankets, clothing, feathers, and leaves. These people later came to America and brought with them their quilting practices.

1. In what ways have people used quilts over the years?

   _____
   _____

2. If Mrs. Crow creates a square quilt from 25 equal-sized patches measuring five inches on a side, what would be the perimeter of the quilt?

   _____
   _____

3. What are some of the items used for stuffing in quilts in 17th-century England?

   _____
   _____
   _____

YOUR TURN

Application

Read the article below. Then answer the questions.

Amish Quilt Style

When most people think of Amish quilts, they think of a quilt that is colorful and richly detailed. In fact, Amish quilts are so wonderfully detailed that they are highly prized by collectors.

Amish quilts are stitched by groups of Amish women and girls. The quilts show beautiful patterns and many different colors, including red, white, green, pink, and blue. Each pattern is carefully stitched by hand. Amish quilts are also very practical and of a very high quality. They can last for decades. However, Amish quilts cannot have any symbols or logos, because such features are considered too fancy and prideful.

Generally, the Amish have a strong belief in working hard and living in simple ways. The process of creating a quilt matches their beliefs. When Amish women and girls gather in a group to stitch a quilt, it strengthens their friendships and their sense of family. They often spend hours working on a single quilt. When the quilt is complete, it is usually sold to a collector or a tourist.

Fluency Tip
Divide longer sentences into phrases. Read each phrase as a short sentence. Then reread the sentence.

1. A quilter has a rectangular quilt. She wants to sew a decorative line along each line of symmetry in the quilt. How many lines of symmetry does the quilt have?

   _____

2. What colors would you expect to see on an Amish quilt?

   _____
   _____
   _____

3. Do you think Amish quilts should have symbols? Why or why not?

   _____
   _____
   _____

Unit 6, Lesson 18

Reading Comprehension

READ on Your Own

Reading Comprehension Strategy: Visualizing

Artworks, pages 33–35

Fluency Tip

As you read and reread, pay attention to punctuation marks that are clues to correct phrasing.

Before You Read

Think about what you read in "Egyptian Art." What was frontalism?

As You Read

Read "Quilting," pages 33–35.

Then use what you have learned to organize facts about how quilting has changed over time. Use the concept map to organize the facts.

- Quilting began with soldiers who needed to keep warm.
- In Colonial times,

Quilting

After You Read

Where have you seen a quilt displayed? What type of pattern did it have?

_____
_____
_____

148   Unit 6, Lesson 18

Problem Solving

SOLVE on Your Own

Artworks, *page 36*

Organize the Information

Read the Math Project in the magazine. Then complete the table to classify shapes by how many lines of symmetry they have.

1 line of symmetry	2 lines of symmetry	3 or more lines of symmetry
isosceles triangle	rectangle	square
_____	_____	_____
_____	_____	_____
_____	_____	_____

Math Project

Use the information in the table above to answer these questions. Write your answers in the space provided.

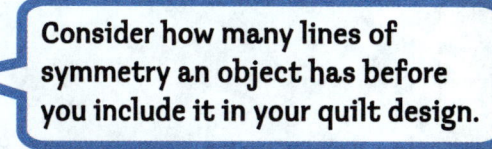

> Consider how many lines of symmetry an object has before you include it in your quilt design.

1. Which polygons are easiest to use in a symmetrical design? Which are the most difficult?

   _____
   _____
   _____

2. When you focus on designing symmetrical quilt blocks, is it easier to have a greater or fewer number of polygons in the design? Why?

   _____
   _____
   _____

After You Solve

Why might it be difficult to cut out the shapes in fabric when assembling a quilt?

_____

Unit 6, Lesson 18

Connections

Put It Together

Introducing Defining Two-Dimensional Space

Have you ever tried to give directions from your school to the library or a friend's house? Sometimes it is difficult to give clear directions. Giving directions in two-dimensional space is sometimes made easier by using a grid like the one shown below.

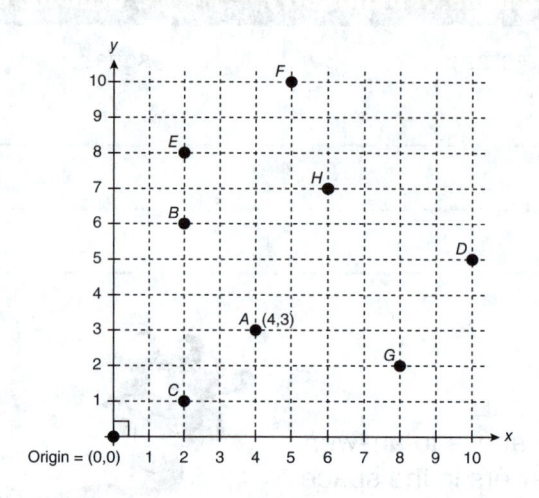

The bottom ray is called the *x*-axis. The ray at the left of the grid is called the *y*-axis. The starting point, the intersection of the two rays in the lower left corner, is called the origin. *Origin* is another word for *beginning*. Any point on the grid can be described with a pair of numbers, (*x, y*). The first number in the pair, the *x*-value, tells you how far to move along the *x*-axis. The second number in the pair, the *y*-value, tells you how far to move along the *y*-axis. The origin is at (0, 0).

To graph or locate the point (4, 3), start at the origin, move 4 units to the right, and then move 3 units up. This point has been marked point A on the grid.

Practicing Defining Two-Dimensional Space

Find the letter that represents each ordered pair.

1. (2, 6) _____
2. (10, 5) _____
3. (6, 7) _____

Give the ordered pair for the letter.

4. Point C _____
5. Point G _____
6. Point F _____

YOUR TURN

Connections

Thinking About Defining Two-Dimensional Space

A grid can help you describe some two-dimensional figures and discover interesting patterns. The points (2, 2), (3, 3), (4, 4), (5, 5) have been graphed on the grid below. Do you see the line pattern? What happens if you graph (6, 6), (7, 7), and (8, 8)?

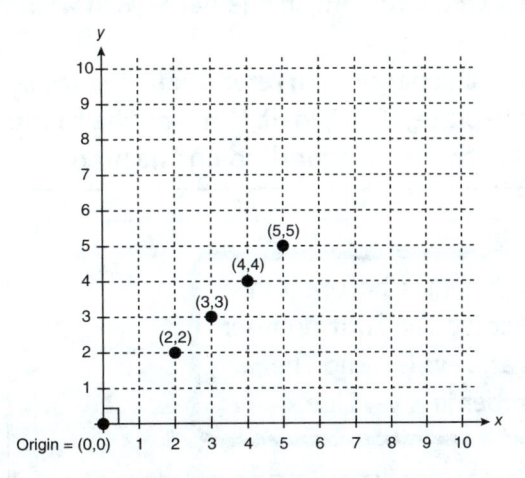

The line pattern continues. Any point that has the same *x*- and *y*-values can be found on this line.

1. Is the point (5, 6) the same as the point (6, 5)?
   _____
   _____

2. How would you explain where to find (0, 8)?
   _____

3. How can you describe the point 7 units up and 6 units to the right?
   _____

4. What is the *y*-value for all points on the *x*-axis? _____

5. Draw a square and write the four vertices as ordered pairs. What number pattern do you see?
   _____

Tip The *x*-values increase as you move to the right. The *y*-values increase as you move up.

Unit 6, Lesson 19   151

Connections

Show That You Know

Read the information below. Use what you know about two-dimensional space to answer the questions that follow. Write your answer to each problem in the space provided.

> Kris and Ryan are helping their mother plan a birthday party for their younger brother, Kyle. Kyle thinks it would be fun to have a treasure hunt in the back yard with his friends. Kris and Ryan are in charge of hiding the treasure.
> They decide to give each child at the party a different set of clues to follow to find their treasure. Each child will start at the same place, (0, 0), visit three of the four points on the map, and find their treasure at a surprise point that is not marked on the map.

Remember: X comes before Y in the alphabet, so the first number in a pair is an *x*-value and the second number is a *y*-value.

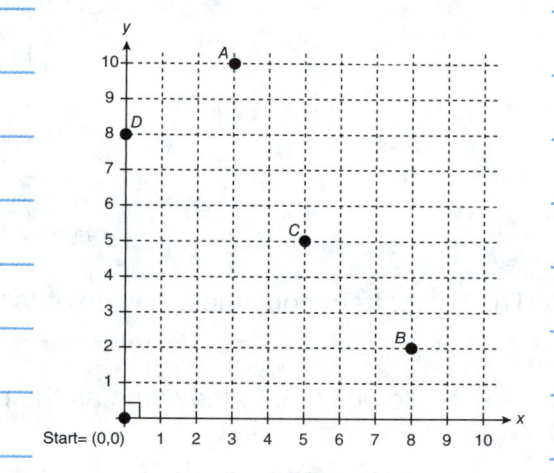

Kris wrote the following directions:

1. Start at (0, 0). Walk to point (8, 2). What point is this?

2. From this point, go up 8 units and 5 units to the left. What point are you at now?

3. Now go 3 units to the left and down 2 units. What point are you at now?

4. Finally, go down 3 units and 3 units to the right. What are the coordinates of your treasure?

5. What are the coordinates of points A, B, C and D?

6. What directions would you give to go from Point B to Point C?

Connections

Show That You Know (continued)

7. Use the grid to write directions to two different treasures. Remember these rules:

   • Each set of directions starts at (0,0).

   • Each child visits three of the lettered points on the map.

   • The final treasure is at a different point for each map.

Treasure Map #1	Treasure Map #2

Review What You've Learned

8. What have you learned in this Connections lesson about naming points on a two-dimensional grid?
   _____
   _____

9. What have you learned in this Connections lesson that you did not already know?
   _____
   _____

10. How will this lesson help you give directions on grid maps?
    _____
    _____

Unit 6, Lesson 19

Review and Practice

Skills Review

Decomposing and combining polygons

Decompose a polygon by breaking it into rectangles and triangles.

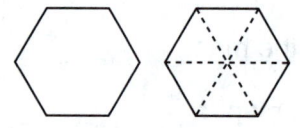

Combine simple polygons to make new shapes.

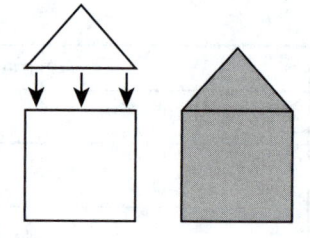

Transformation of polygons

Translations and rotations can be used to line up the congruent parts of congruent figures.

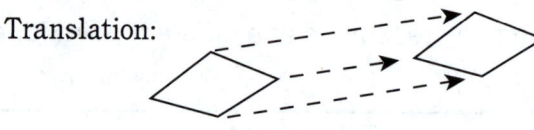

Translation:

Rotation:

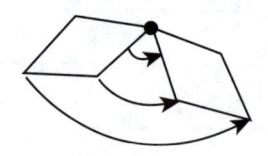

Complementary and supplementary angles

A 90° angle is a right angle. Two angles whose measures add to 90° are complementary angles. A 180° angle is a straight angle. Two angles whose measures add to 180° are supplementary angles.

Forming triangles

Three lines can be joined to make a triangle if the sum of the lengths of any two of those lines is greater than the length of the third line.

Congruent figures

Congruent figures have the same shape and size. A square or rectangle can be decomposed into two congruent triangles. The triangles have the same shape and size.

Lines of symmetry

Lines of symmetry divide a shape into two congruent shapes that are a mirror image of one another.

Strategy Review

- When you are combining polygons to form complex polygons, you can draw the polygons on paper, cut them out, and fit them together to see how they will look. This also makes transformations easier.

- If you use a ruler and protractor to draw shapes on paper and cut them out, you can use these polygons to find complementary angles and supplementary angles.

- To find the lines of symmetry in a polygon, you can draw the shape on paper then fold it in half. You can also use a mirror. If the two halves match exactly, it is a line of symmetry. A shape can have more than one line of symmetry.

Review and Practice

Skills and Strategies Practice

Complete the exercises below.

1. If you decompose a regular octagon into congruent triangles, how many triangles would you get?
   _____

2. What transformation is shown?

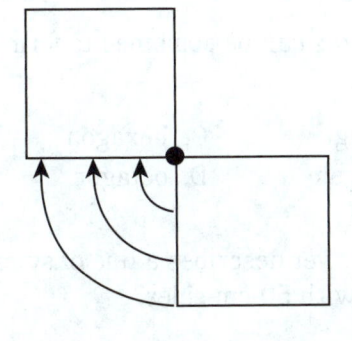

   _____

3. If the sum of two sides of a triangle is 10 inches, what is true of the third side?
   _____

4. Which pair of angles are complementary angles?

   90°, 45°

   45°, 45°

   46°, 134°
   _____

5. Look at the figure below.

   Are the triangles congruent? Why or why not?
   _____
   _____
   _____
   _____

6. Which pair of angles are supplementary angles?

   90°, 45°

   45°, 45°

   46°, 134°
   _____

Test-Taking tip: It is easier to learn new vocabulary words if you make them part of your speaking and writing in other discussions and subject areas. Practice describing objects and shapes around your school or home to others while using vocabulary words. For example, use *rotate, symmetry, congruent, right triangle, complementary,* and *supplementary.*

Unit 6, Lesson 20

Review and Practice

Unit Review

Circle the letter of the correct answer.

1. Which shape can be easily decomposed into two congruent triangles?

    A. square C. trapezoid
    B. circle D. pentagon

2. Which angle is supplementary to a 97° angle?

    A. 3° angle C. 7° angle
    B. 83° angle D. 97° angle

3. Look at the shape below.

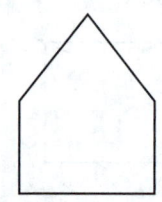

    This pentagon can be decomposed into what two shapes?
    A. two triangles
    B. a triangle and a circle
    C. two parallelograms
    D. a triangle and a square

4. What larger shape can you make if you combine these smaller shapes?

    A. a pentagon C. a trapezoid
    B. an octagon D. a circle

5.

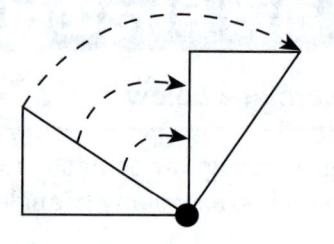

    This diagram shows a _____.
    A. translation
    B. rotation
    C. line of symmetry
    D. pair of supplementary angles

6. Two squares can be combined to form which shape?

    A. rectangle C. hexagon
    B. pentagon D. octagon

7. Which answer describes a line of symmetry on a square with 50-cm sides?

    A. a diagonal line from the upper right corner to the lower left corner
    B. a vertical line 20 cm from the left
    C. a vertical line 30 cm from the left
    D. a horizontal line 10 cm from the bottom

8.

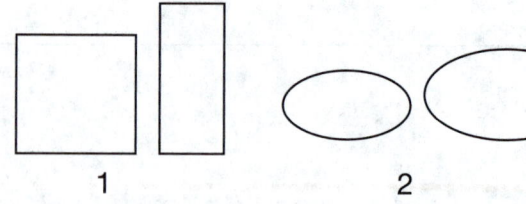

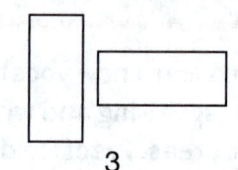

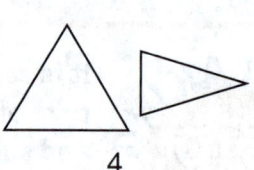

    Which pair of shapes is congruent?
    A. 1   B. 2   C. 3   D. 4

156 Unit 6, Lesson 20

Review and Practice

9. Six congruent triangles can be combined to create which shape?

    A. a hexagon   C. a pentagon
    B. a rectangle   D. a square

10. Which angle could be used with a 111° angle to form a straight angle?

    A. 21° angle   C. 59° angle
    B. 79° angle   D. 69° angle

11.

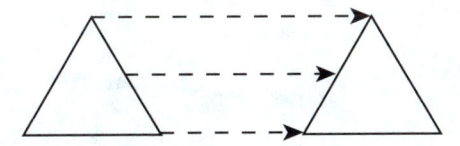

    This diagram shows a _____.
    A. rotation to the right
    B. rotation to the left
    C. translation to the right
    D. translation to the left

12. Which shape can be broken into one rectangle and two triangles, or six triangles?

    A. an octagon   C. a hexagon
    B. a pentagon   D. a square

13. Which angle is complementary to a 13° angle?

    A. 167° angle   C. 103° angle
    B. 157° angle   D. 77° angle

14. Which side lengths can be used to draw a triangle?

    A. 3, 3, 7   C. 4, 4, 6
    B. 4, 2, 1   D. 2, 5, 1

15. Two congruent triangles will have the same _____.

    A. size
    B. size, shape, and angle measurements
    C. shape
    D. angle measurements

16.

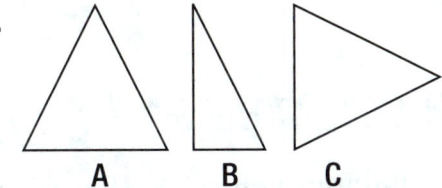

    A   B   C

    Which triangles are congruent?
    A. A, B, and C   C. A and B
    B. B and C   D. A and C

17. Which angles are complementary angles?

    A. 90°, 45°   C. 30°, 60°
    B. 45°, 47°   D. 33°, 150°

18. Which angle would need to be added to a 123° angle to make a straight angle?

    A. 57°   B. 47°   C. 97°   D. 119°

19. If two sides of a triangle are 6 and 14, how long might the third side be?

    A. 11   B. 7   C. 32   D. 20

20. Which shape can be most easily broken down into one rectangle and four triangles, or six triangles?

    A. pentagon   C. heptagon
    B. triangle   D. octagon

Unit 6, Lesson 20

Unit 6 Reflection

MATH SKILLS

The difference between a square and a rectangle is

I can decompose a rectangle into

MATH STRATEGIES & CONNECTIONS

When combining shapes, the math strategy that works for me is

I know a shape is not a polygon when

READING STRATEGIES & COMPREHENSION

The easiest part about visualizing is

One way that visualizing helps me with reading is

The vocabulary words I had trouble with are

INDEPENDENT READING

One thing I learned about art was

My favorite article in <u>Artworks</u> was

Artworks

UNIT 7
Area of Two-Dimensional Shapes

MATH SKILLS & STRATEGIES
After you learn the basic **SKILLS**, the real test is knowing when to use each **STRATEGY**.

AMP LINK MAGAZINE
You Do the Math and Math Projects: After you read each magazine article, apply what you know in real-world problems.
Fluency: Make your reading smooth and accurate, one tip at a time.

READING STRATEGY
Use **Metacognition:** knowing how and when to use Reading Comprehension Strategies.

CONNECTIONS
You own the math when you make your own connections.

VOCABULARY
MATH WORDS:
Know them!
Use them!
Learn all about them!

Reading Comprehension Strategy

Reading Comprehension Strategy: Metacognition

What good readers do

Before Reading	During Reading	After Reading
• Preview • Think about the topic • Ask questions • Make predictions	• Identify the topic, main idea, and details • Identify the text structure, ask questions, visualize • Reread	• Summarize • Ask questions • Use graphic organizers to arrange information

Step 1: Before Reading

Metacognition pulls together all the reading strategies you have learned about. When you use metacognition, you think about how you are reading. You plan the best way to get information. You check to see if you understand what you read. You also look for answers to your questions. Prepare to read this article about an ancient Aztec city.

Step 2: During Reading

Good readers think about which strategies to use as they read. They preview the paragraph before they read it. They think about the kinds of questions they can ask to understand what they read. They look for the text structure signals. They find important details and use them to visualize what they are reading.

Lucia looked north and saw the Pyramid of the Moon. In the bright sun, its rough stones looked white. Lucia knew that the smaller pyramid had once been painted red. She imagined how it might have looked against the green mountains in the distance.

Lucia wanted to explore the rest of Mexico's ancient ruined city, Teotihuacán (tay oh tee wah KAHN). Going up the steps had been easy. Now, however, the stairs seemed to be going straight down. Lucia did what the guide had said. She kept her eyes on the step in front of her. She did not look at anything else.

At the bottom of the stairs, Lucia turned south. She walked down a wide road toward a large square courtyard. Inside was the Temple of the Feathered Serpent. Lucia knew he was the sky god worshipped by the ancient Aztecs. She walked into the temple and went around a sacred stone table. Then she came to another altar with many carvings of the sky god.

---

1. Which strategies did you use to prepare to read the article? Describe how you used one of the strategies.
   ☐ Preview
   ☐ Think about the topic
   ☐ Ask questions
   ☐ Make predictions
   _____
   _____

2. What is a question you could ask to understand the second paragraph?
   _____
   _____
   _____

Reading Comprehension Strategy

Step 3: After Reading

When you have finished reading, ask yourself, *Do I need to reread to find answers to my questions? How might a graphic organizer help me better understand what I have read? What important details would go in a summary of this article?*

Once your questions are answered, see if you can summarize what you have read. Use your own words or a graphic organizer.

> Flecks of the green paint showed that the carvings had once been painted green. Lucia tried to picture what they had looked like. She remembered what her people, the Aztecs, said when they found the ruins of Teotihuacán. They thought it was a holy place and called it "the City of the Gods," which it is still called today.

3. After reading this paragraph, Lee could not remember how to pronounce *Teotihuacán*. What should Lee do to find out?

   _____
   _____
   _____
   _____
   _____

4. Summarize the places Lucia saw while exploring.

   _____
   _____
   _____
   _____
   _____
   _____
   _____

The view from the Pyramid of the Moon in Teotihuacán includes the enormous Temple of the Sun.

5. What is a benefit of using the Metacognition reading comprehension strategy?
   _____
   _____
   _____

6. What questions do you have about how to use metacognition?
   _____
   _____
   _____

Unit 7   161

Use the Strategies

Use the reading comprehension strategies you have learned to answer questions about the article below.

The End of Pompeii

On August 24 in A.D. 79, the people of Pompeii were going about their daily business. Around noon, Mount Vesuvius erupted. The volcano threw dust, ashes, and rocks high into the air. By late afternoon, the cloud rose so high that it blocked out the sun.

A constant rain of rocks fell on Pompeii. The rocks that landed on the houses caused many roofs to collapse. Poisonous gases began to settle over the city. Within eight hours of the eruption, Pompeii was buried.

By dawn on August 25, hot steam and mud had flowed down the side of Vesuvius. The town of Herculaneum, four miles away from Vesuvius, was covered. That morning, the last surges of the volcano struck and buried Pompeii. When the final volcanic surge hit at 8:00 A.M., the flow collapsed the highest walls of the buildings. By midday on August 25, Pompeii was gone.

Archaeologists, or scientists who study the ruins of past cultures, have explored the ruins of Pompeii and learned many things about what life was like in ancient Rome. They uncovered beautiful houses. They also found the remains of people who were caught and died in the eruption. Many of them were holding their most prized possessions.

Archaeologists also found many surviving frescoes and mosaics. Frescoes are pictures painted on walls. Mosaics are designs made from very small tiles. One mosaic at the entrance to a house shows a snarling dog. Archaeologists believe this sign warned visitors to "Beware of the Dog!"

1. What clues in the first paragraph tell you that the information is presented in chronological order?
   _____
   _____
   _____
   _____

2. Contrast what happened to Herculaneum and Pompeii.
   _____
   _____
   _____
   _____
   _____
   _____

3. What have archaeologists found in Pompeii?
   _____
   _____
   _____
   _____

4. What do you think the mosaic of the dog looks like? What helped you visualize the mosaic?
   _____
   _____
   _____
   _____
   _____
   _____

Use the Strategies

Reading Comprehension Strategy: Visualizing, Text Structure, Metacognition

Use the reading comprehension strategies you have learned in this and previous units to answer the questions below.

1. Write one example of cause and effect from this article. Explain how you recognized this text structure.
   _____
   _____

2. Make a flowchart showing the order of events in Pompeii. Use the space below.

Problem-Solving Strategies:
Try a Simpler Form of the Problem, Make a Table or a Chart

Use these problem-solving strategies to answer the questions below.

3. How long was it from the first eruption of Vesuvius to the start of the final surge? In other words, how many hours were there from noon on the first day to 8:00 A.M. on the second day? Use the Try a Simpler Form of the Problem strategy to find how much time had passed.
   _____
   _____

4. If Mt. Vesuvius released 5 tons of rock per second, how many tons of rock were released in five minutes? Use the Make a Table or a Chart strategy to find the answer.
   _____

5. Continue the table to find out how many tons were released in 10 minutes.
   _____
   _____

Unit 7   163

Learn the Skill

Area

Learn the SKILL

Ellen has a garden that is the shape of a rectangle. She wants to know the exact area of this garden. One side is 4 feet long and the other is 7 feet long. How can she find the area of her garden?

VOCABULARY

Watch for the words you are learning about.

area: the number of square units enclosed by a region

base: a side of a polygon; length

height: the distance from top to bottom; width

square unit: a square with sides 1 unit long used to measure area

unit: one of the parts into which a whole can be analyzed

unit square: a square with sides that are 1 unit in length and having an area of 1 square unit

SKILL	EXAMPLE	WRITE AN EXAMPLE
Area is the number of square units needed to cover a region. A grid can be placed over a region to show how many square units it covers. Each square, a **unit square**, represents 1 unit of area, or 1 **square unit**.	Find the area of a rectangle that is 4 units by 7 units. 7 units 4 units There are 28 squares so the area is 28 square units.	Draw and label the dimensions of a rectangle with an area of 12 square units.
One side of this shape, or rectangle, is called the **base** or length. The distance from top to bottom is called the **height** or width.	Identify the base and the height of the following rectangle. 7 units 10 units The height is 7 units and the base is 10 units.	Draw and label a rectangle. Indicate its base and height.
The area of a rectangle can be found by multiplying the base by the height: $A = b \times h$.	What is the area of a rectangle with a base of 7 units and a height of 4 units? $A = b \times h = 7 \times 4 = 28$ square units	What is the area of a rectangle with a base of 2 units and height of 8 units?

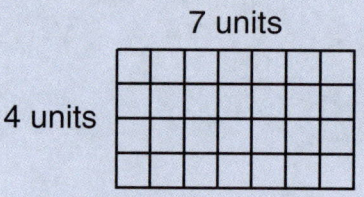

Unit 7, Lesson 1

YOUR TURN

Choose the Right Word

area   base   height   unit

Fill in each blank with the correct word or phrase from the box.

1. A(n) _____ is a part into which a whole can be analyzed.

2. The _____ is the distance from top to bottom.

3. The _____ of a figure is the number of square units it encloses.

4. The _____ is the side of a polygon at the bottom.

Yes or No?

Answer these questions and be ready to explain your answers.

5. In a square, does the height equal the base? _____

6. Does the height always equal the base in a rectangle? _____

7. Is the area of a rectangle calculated by adding the base to the height? _____

8. Can area be calculated by counting the unit squares that make up a figure? _____

Show That You Know

Find the area by drawing the rectangle and using a grid.

9. 9 units by 2 units

10. 4 units by 12 units

Identify the height and the base.

11. length = 4 units
    width = 1 unit

    height =

    base =

Find the area.

12. base: 1 unit
    height: 8 units

13. base: 3 units
    height: 4 units

Unit 7, Lesson 1   165

Learn the Skill

SOLVE on Your Own

Skills Practice

Remember to include square units in your answers.

Find the area by drawing the figure, making a grid, and counting the units.

1. 7 units by 4 units
2. 9 units by 1 unit
3. 5 units by 5 units

Identify the base and the height.

4. _____

length = 10 units
width = 2 units

5. _____

length = 8 units
width = 3 units

Calculate the area.

6. base = 10 units, height = 6 units

7. base = 4 units, height = 5 units

8. base = 5 units, height = 9 units

9. square with each side measuring 1 unit

10. base = 9 units, height = 2 units

11. base = 4 units, height = 8 units

12. base = 3 units, height = 7 units

Unit 7, Lesson 1

Choose a Strategy

Area
Strategy
Draw a Picture or Use a Model

Step 1: Read You want to build a rectangular patio in the backyard using paving stones that measure 1 foot by 1 foot. The length of the patio will be 20 feet. The width of the patio will be 14 feet. However, there is a tree growing at the top edge of the space where you want the patio to go. You want the tree to be in the center at the top edge of the patio, so you must leave a 4-foot by 4-foot unpaved opening for the tree. How many paving stones will you need?

STRATEGY	SOLUTION
Draw a Picture or Use a Model Draw a picture of the shape of the patio. Label the dimensions and multiply to find the area. Since the paving stones are 1 foot by 1 foot, the area will be equal to the number of paving stones needed.	**Step 2: Plan** Draw the figure from the problem. Using dashed lines, divide the figure into smaller figures. Find the area of each smaller figure and combine for the area of the whole figure. **Step 3: Solve** Draw and label a rectangle with the dimensions given. Make a mark halfway across the length on one edge. Draw a box at this center point and label it 4 feet by 4 feet. Erase the outside edge of the box, leaving a shape that looks like the shape below.

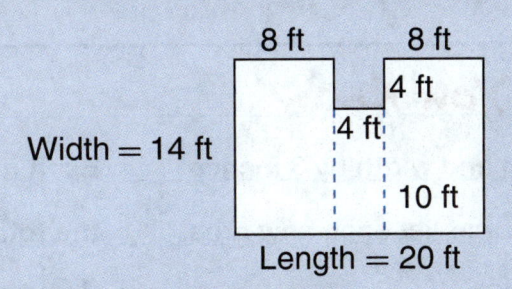

```
        8 ft      8 ft
                 4 ft
              4 ft
Width = 14 ft
                 10 ft
        Length = 20 ft
```

Use dashed lines to divide the figure into three rectangles. Subtract to find the dimensions of each side of each new figure.

14 feet − 4 feet = 10 feet   20 feet − 4 feet = 16 feet

The remaining length must be divided into two parts. 16 feet ÷ 2 = 8 feet

To find the total area, find the area of each rectangle and add.

8 feet × 14 feet = 112 feet^2

8 feet × 14 feet = 112 feet^2

4 feet × 10 feet = 40 feet^2

112 feet^2 + 112 feet^2 + 40 feet^2 = 264 feet^2

You will need 264 paving stones.

Step 4: Check Use one-inch squares or pieces of paper to build a model of the patio.

YOUR TURN

Choose the Right Word

> area length square width

Fill in each blank with the correct word or phrase from the box.

1. The measurement of the space inside a figure is called its _____.

2. A(n) _____ has the same measures for its length and width.

3. To find the area of a rectangle, you must multiply the _____ and the _____.

Yes or No?

Answer these questions and be ready to explain your answers.

4. To find the area of complex figures should you first split the area into other polygons? _____

5. If one dimension of an object increases, will the area increase? _____

6. If one dimension of an object decreases, is the area greater? _____

7. Is the result the same whether you multiply the length by the width or the width by the length? _____

Show That You Know

Increase each length and width by 3 inches three different times and list each new area.

8. 5 in. × 7 in. = 35 in.²

9. 16 in. × 11 in. = 176 in.²

Each figure is made of two rectangles. Find the total area of each figure.

10. 10 in. × 13 in. and 11 in. × 6 in.

11. 13 yd × 6 yd and 23 yd × 13 yd

Unit 7, Lesson 2

READ on Your Own

Reading Comprehension Strategy: Metacognition

Ancient Cultures, *pages 3–4*

Before You Read

Think about the traditions practiced where you live. Which ones are most important to you?

As You Read

Read "Modern Roots in Mayan Culture," pages 3–4.

Then read the statements below. Are they true or false? Write *T* for true or *F* for false.

Mayan Culture	True or False?
The Maya did not know how to write or how to do math.	
The Maya built pyramids.	
Men and women were both allowed to play pitz.	
All the Great Ball Courts were the same size.	

After You Read

What games do you play that might be similar to the game of pitz?

_____

_____

VOCABULARY

Watch for the words you are learning about.

cultures: ways of life, traditions, and customs of groups of people

pyramids: buildings with square bases and four sides shaped like triangles

society: a group of people who live in the same area and share laws and customs

structure: something that is built, such as a building or a bridge

Fluency Tip

Review any words in boldfaced type before you read. Make sure you know how to pronounce these words.

Problem Solving

SOLVE on Your Own

Ancient Cultures, page 5

Organize the Information

Read You Do the Math in the magazine. Then fill out the table below with information on a football field and the Great Ball Court at Chichén Itzá.

Playing Field	Shape	Length	Width	Area
football field				
Great Ball Court				

You Do the Math

Use the information in the table above and in the magazine to answer these questions. Write your answers in the space provided.

Drawing a picture of the playing areas may help you answer the magazine questions.

1. How did you find the area of the football field?

   _____
   _____

2. How did you find the area of the Great Ball Court at Chichén Itzá?

   _____
   _____
   _____
   _____

After You Solve

The Great Ball Courts were in the shape of the letter **I**. What are the shapes of some modern sports playing areas?

_____
_____

Unit 7, Lesson 2

Learn the Skill

Area Units

Learn the SKILL

Jamal has a piece of paper. He wants to find the area of the piece of paper in different square units. What square units of measure can he use?

SKILL	EXAMPLE	WRITE AN EXAMPLE
As you learned earlier, area can be found by counting the number of squares that make up the shape. The area is then expressed as square units or units².	Find the area of a rectangle that is 6 units wide by 4 units long. length = 4 units width = 6 units 6 units × 4 units = 24 square units	Draw and label a square and its sides in units. Find the area of your square. Use units² in your answer. _____
Measurements of rectangles might be expressed in inches (in.), feet (ft), yards (yd), meters (m), or some other unit of length. All the answers are expressed as square units of that measurement.	Find the area of a rectangle that is 6 inches wide by 4 inches long. length = 4 inches width = 6 inches $A = 6$ in. $\times 4$ in. $= 24$ in.² Find the area of a square with a side measuring 5 feet. $A = 5$ ft $\times 5$ ft $= 25$ ft²	Give dimensions for a rectangle with sides measuring between 2 yards and 5 yards. _____ What is the area in square yards? _____
Sometimes, the dimensions of a figure are given in different units of measure. These must be converted to similar units: 12 in. = 1 ft and 3 ft = 1 yd	Find the area of a rectangle that is 12 in. by 3 ft. Hint: 12 in. = 1 ft $A = 1$ ft $\times 3$ ft $= 3$ ft² or $A = 12$ in. $\times 36$ in. $= 432$ in.²	Find the area of your rectangle in square feet. _____

Unit 7, Lesson 3

Learn the Skill

YOUR TURN

Choose the Right Word

area   base   height   unit

Fill in each blank with the correct word or phrase from the box.

1. The _____ is the side of a polygon that is horizontal and at the bottom.

2. The _____ of a figure is the number of square units it encloses.

3. A(n) _____ is a part into which a whole can be analyzed.

4. The _____ is the distance from top of a figure to the bottom.

Yes or No?

Answer these questions and be ready to explain your answers.

5. Are 12 feet equal to 1 inch? _____

6. Are 24 inches equal to 2 feet? _____

7. If a rectangle were measured in meters, would the area be expressed as meters^2? _____

8. If the dimensions are measured in feet, could the area be calculated in square inches? _____

Show That You Know

Find the area of each rectangle or write "not possible." Convert units if necessary.

9. 9 units long by 2 units wide

10. 4 ft long by 12 in. wide

11. 12 in. long by 2 in. wide

12. 4 units wide by 1 in. long

13. 1 ft wide by 8 ft long

14. 3 m wide by 4 m long

15. 0 m wide by 4 m long

172   Unit 7, Lesson 3

SOLVE on Your Own

Skills Practice

Remember to convert units if necessary.

Find each area and write it on the line.

1. 8 units long by 4 units wide _____

2. 9 in. long by 1 in. wide _____

3. 5 in. wide by 1 ft long _____

4. 10 ft long by 5 ft wide _____

5. 8 yd long by 6 ft wide _____

6. 7 m long by 4 m wide _____

7. 6 cm wide by 11 cm long _____

8. 6 ft long by 12 in. wide _____

9. a square with a one-inch side _____

10. 19 units long by 2 units wide _____

11. 1 in. wide by 2 in. long _____

12. 36 in. wide by 3 ft long _____

Choose a Strategy

Area Units
Strategies
Make a Table or a Chart,
Draw a Picture or Use a Model

Step 1: Read You have to build a square pyramid five levels high out of sugar cubes for history class. The area of each sugar cube is 1 cm². The bottom level will have an area of 225 cm². The top (and smallest) level will have an area of 121 cm². What are the lengths and widths of each level if they both increase by 1 from the top down? What are their areas?

STRATEGY	SOLUTION
Make a Table or a Chart Different lengths, widths, and areas can be organized in a table.	**Step 2: Plan** Draw a table with three columns and six rows. Label the columns "Length," "Width," and "Area." In the first empty box under the "Area" label, write "225 cm²." In the last box under the "Area" label, write "121 cm²." Fill in the missing lengths, widths, and areas. **Step 3: Solve** Since each square level of the pyramid is made of squares, you can find the dimensions of bottom and top levels. What number multiplied by itself gives you 225? Combine your strategy with the Guess, Check, and Revise strategy to solve. The answer is 15 cubes. Write "15 cm" in the length and width columns. What number multiplied by itself gives you 121? Again, combine your strategy with the Guess, Check, and Revise strategy to solve. The answer is 11 cubes. Write "11 cm" in the length and width columns. Since there are five levels to the pyramid, you can decrease the number of cubes by one for each level and write the new length and width in the columns: 15, 14, 13, 12, and 11. Multiply each length by itself to find the area for each level: 225 cm², 196 cm², 169 cm², 144 cm², and 121 cm². **Step 4: Check** Use cubes to make a physical model of each level of the pyramid.
Draw a Picture or Use a Model Using blocks, you can make a model of the pyramid to solve the problem.	**Step 2: Plan** Arrange 225 blocks into a square. How many blocks are on each side? Use this strategy to find the remaining dimensions. **Step 3: Solve** Make a square of blocks on top of the first square that has sides that measure 1 unit less in length. Multiply the length and width to find the area. Continue adding layers of squares of blocks until all five layers of the pyramid are built. The top layer should have 121 blocks. **Step 4: Check** Count the number of blocks in each level to check the area of each level.

YOUR TURN

Choose the Right Word

area   height   square units

Fill in each blank with the correct word or phrase from the box.

1. The _____ of a rectangle is also known as its "width."

2. To find the _____ of a square, multiply its length by width.

3. Area is measured in _____.

Choose a Strategy

Yes or No?

Answer these questions and be ready to explain your answers.

4. When you are finding area, do you square the units? _____

5. If rectangle 1 has a length and width less than rectangle 2, will rectangle 2 have a greater area? _____

6. To find the area, do you add the length and width? _____

7. Is a 2 inch by 2 inch square a unit square? _____

Show That You Know

Find the area of a square with sides that measure the given lengths.

8. 40 inches

9. 15 feet

10. 25 meters

Find the area of each rectangle. Then order the rectangles from least to greatest area.

11. Rectangle 1 = 45 feet × 9 feet

    Rectangle 2 = 8 feet × 88 feet

    Rectangle 3 = 29 feet × 16 feet

Unit 7, Lesson 4   175

Reading Comprehension

READ on Your Own

Reading Comprehension Strategy: Metacognition

Ancient Cultures, pages 6–7

Before You Read

When you read "Modern Roots in Mayan Culture," you learned about traditions, buildings, and games that were important to the Maya. Which buildings are important to you today?

As You Read

Read "Built to Last Centuries," pages 6–7. 🛑

Then read the statements in the left column. Are they true or false? Write T for true or F for false in the right column.

Mayan Architecture	True or False?
You cannot learn anything about ancient Mexico by looking at the architecture.	
Jewelry found at Chichén Itzá tell archaeologists that the Maya were wealthy.	
The long noses on the tops of many Mayan buildings represented their gods.	
The Maya built pyramids to worship their gods.	
The Temple of the Warriors showed other nations how beautiful Mayan art was.	

VOCABULARY

Watch for the words you are learning about.

archaeologists: people who study how ancient people lived

architecture: the art or science of designing and building structures

artifacts: objects, such as tools, made or changed by people in the past

columns: cylinder-shaped building supports

Fluency Tip

Review any words in boldfaced type before you read. Make sure you know how to pronounce these words.

After You Read

Many important buildings have columns. What famous buildings do you know about that have columns?

_____

_____

Problem Solving

SOLVE on Your Own

Ancient Cultures, *page 8*

Organize the Information

Read You Do the Math in the magazine. Then fill out the table below with information on the dimensions and areas of El Castillo and your model.

	El Castillo			Your Model		
	Length	Width	Area	Length	Width	Area
Base						
Temple						

You Do the Math

Use the information in the table above to answer these questions. Write your answers in the space provided.

Use what you know about meters and centimeters to help you find the measurements of your model.

1. How did you find the area of the base of El Castillo?
   _____
   _____

2. How do the areas of El Castillo and the areas in your model compare? Explain your answer.
   _____
   _____
   _____

After You Solve

Do you think the Maya were ahead of their time? Why or why not?
_____
_____

Unit 7, Lesson 4

Application

Solve It!

The Four-Step Problem-Solving Plan

Step 1: Read	Step 2: Plan	Step 3: Solve	Step 4: Check
Make sure you understand what the problem is asking.	Decide how you will solve the problem.	Solve the problem using your plan.	Check to make sure your answer is correct.

Read the article below. Then answer the questions.

Incan Religion

Before Europeans came to South America, the Inca had unified many people over a large part of the continent. They achieved this by moving conquered people to Incan areas. The Inca then made the people adopt Incan culture as their own. They also unified their empire by requiring everyone to follow the same religion. The religion required people to worship the sun, yet allowed them to continue practicing their original faiths. In other words, people could worship the same way they had before being conquered, as long as they also worshipped the sun.

Many of the ceremonies for the new religion took place in the grounds outside of temple buildings. The insides of the temples were generally too small to hold large groups of worshippers. However, there are exceptions. The ground plan of the Temple of Viracocha at San Pedro Cacha, in Peru, measured 330 feet by 87 feet. This suggests that the building was meant for more than just storage. Possibly, people of many backgrounds united by Incan culture worshiped in this temple.

1. Summarize the main idea of the first paragraph.

   _____
   _____
   _____
   _____
   _____

2. What was the area of the Temple of Viracocha?

   _____
   _____

YOUR TURN

Application

Read the article below. Then answer the questions.

Huacas

One of the largest temples was the huge circular Temple of the Sun in Cuzco, which measured about 380 feet across. In addition to these enormous temples, the Inca also worshipped at countless smaller sites known as *huacas.* Huacas could be almost anything—smaller temples, burial sites, bridges, mountains or hills, rivers, waterfalls, or even small piles of stones. Families would even have their own huacas, in the form of small objects or statues, to keep in their homes.

The people who lived close to these sacred sites believed that respect for the sites would bring good fortune. For example, leaving a pebble on a sacred pile of stones at the roadside was considered a prayer for safe travel. Other sites were thought to bring good luck to the traveler in different ways.

Fluency Tip
Remember to read smoothly. Try to read phrases instead of individual words.

1. How could you estimate the area of a place like the Temple of the Sun, which is a circle?

   _____
   _____
   _____
   _____

2. Name one detail you did not know about the Inca before you read this article.

   _____
   _____
   _____
   _____

3. Use your response to question 1 to estimate the area of the Temple of the Sun in Cuzco.

   _____
   _____
   _____
   _____

Unit 7, Lesson 5   179

Reading Comprehension

READ on Your Own

Reading Comprehension Strategy: Metacognition

Ancient Cultures, *pages 9–11*

VOCABULARY

Watch for the words you are learning about.

civilizations: well-developed societies or groups of people

conquered: took over by means of war

observation: the act of noticing or recording an event

Fluency Tip

Divide longer sentences into phrases. Read each phrase as a short sentence. Then reread the sentence.

Before You Read

Consider the Mayan architecture you read about in "Built to Last Centuries." Which Mayan design elements are also part of modern architecture?

As You Read

Preview "Towers to the Sun," pages 9–11. STOP

Check the boxes that apply.

☐ Did you preview the text?
☐ Did you read the title?
☐ Did you look at the pictures?
☐ Did you read the captions?
☐ Did you think about what you already know about the topic?
☐ Did you think about what you would like to learn?
☐ Did you set a goal for reading?

Read pages 9–11. STOP
Answer the questions below.

How did your preview of the pages help you understand them?

_____
_____

What might you do differently before you read next time?

_____
_____

After You Read

How could you find answers to questions that were not answered in the article? Explain your answer.

_____
_____

180   Unit 7, Lesson 5

Problem Solving

SOLVE on Your Own

Ancient Cultures, *page 12*

Organize the Information

Fill in the list below to organize the information you find in the Math Project.

Width of each space: _____

Total width of all 12 spaces: 12 × _____ = _____

Width of 10 towers: 10 × _____ = _____

Width of 3 more towers: 3 × _____ = _____

Total width of all 13 towers: _____

Total width of spaces and towers: _____ + _____ = 300 m

Math Project

Use the information in the list above to answer these questions. Write your answers in the space below.

> Figure out the width of each tower before making your drawing.

1. How can you use the total width of the Thirteen Towers at Chankillo and the width of the twelve spaces to find the total width of the towers?

   _____
   _____

2. How did you choose the width of each tower?

   _____
   _____
   _____
   _____

After You Solve

What math strategies did you use to help you solve the problem?

_____
_____

Unit 7, Lesson 5   181

Learn the Skill

Using the Area Model

Learn the SKILL

Evan has 12 square tiles. He can arrange them all into several different rectangles. How can he compare the area of these figures?

SKILL	EXAMPLE	WRITE AN EXAMPLE
Area models can help explain and explore factors. Two factors of a number can be expressed as the number of units in the base and the number of units in the height of a rectangle.	How many different rectangles can be formed with 12 unit squares? Three different rectangles are shown: 1 × 12, 2 × 6 and 3 × 4. 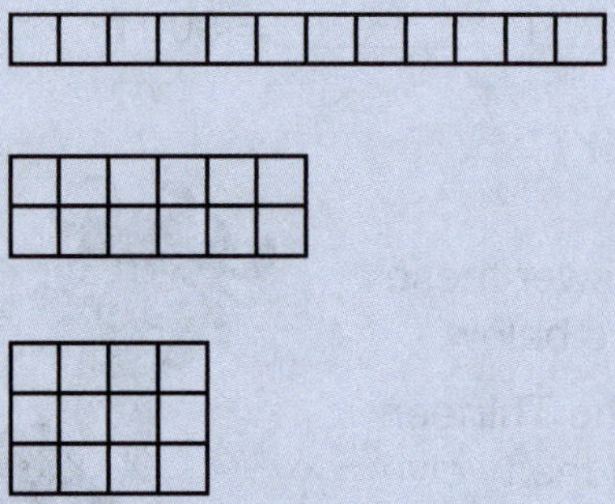 Three more are possible: 12 × 1, 6 × 2 and 4 × 3. All of the rectangles have an area of 12 square units.	Choose a number between 20 and 30. _____ Name all possible area models for your number. _____ _____ How many area models does your number have? _____
Area models are also helpful in explaining multidigit multiplication.	32 × 57 Find the area of each rectangle and add to find the total area. 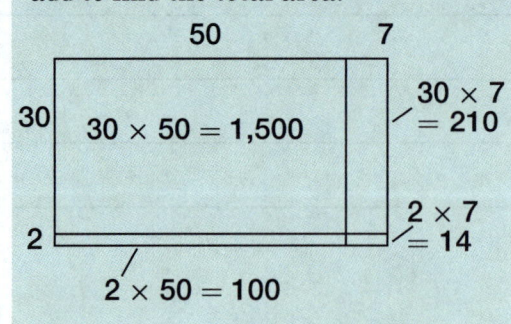 30 × 50 = 1,500 30 × 7 = 210 2 × 50 = 100 2 × 7 = 14 1,500 + 100 + 210 + 14 = 1,824	Write a multiplication expression using two two-digit numbers. _____ Draw an area model to explain the product.

Unit 7, Lesson 6

YOUR TURN

Learn the Skill

Choose the Right Word

> area model   base height   unit

Fill in each blank with the correct word or phrase from the box.

1. The _____ is the distance from top to bottom of a figure.

2. A(n) _____ is a visual way to describe area.

3. The _____ of a rectangle is the same as its length.

4. A(n) _____ is a part into which a whole can be analyzed.

Yes or No?

Answer these questions and be ready to explain your answers.

5. If you know just the area of a rectangle is it possible to determine the height? _____

6. Given the area of a square is it possible to determine the length of one side? _____

7. Can an area model be used to explain multidigit multiplication? _____

8. Is there only one area model for the factors of 7? _____

Show That You Know

Draw area models on a separate sheet of paper to show all possible factors of the number. Then write the factors below.

9. 20

10. 25

11. 11

Draw area models on a separate sheet of paper to help find the products below. Write the product after the expression.

12. 13 × 21

13. 25 × 25

14. 67 × 73

Unit 7, Lesson 6   183

Learn the Skill

SOLVE on Your Own

Skills Practice

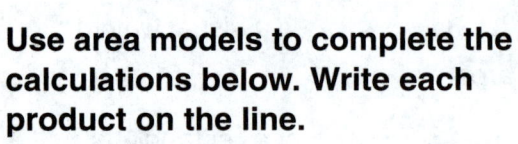

Okay, now you know all about using area models. Show it by completing these exercises.

Use area models to find all the factors of each number. Then list the factors below.

1. 28 _____
   _____

2. 49 _____
   _____

3. 23 _____
   _____

4. 36 _____
   _____
   _____

5. 56 _____
   _____

6. 100 _____
   _____
   _____

Use area models to complete the calculations below. Write each product on the line.

7. 21 × 11 _____

8. 22 × 18 _____

9. 45 × 35 _____

10. 51 × 51 _____

11. 75 × 75 _____

12. 89 × 98 _____

184 Unit 7, Lesson 6

Choose a Strategy

Using the Area Model
Strategies
Make a Table or a Chart,
Draw a Picture or Use a Model

Step 1: Read A construction company wants to build three different houses that each have different dimensions. Each house must measure 45 ft long and must an area greater than 1,000 ft² but less than 2,000 ft². What are three possible dimensions and areas for houses they can build?

STRATEGY	SOLUTION
Make a Table or a Chart Using a table or chart, you can organize your information to determine three different house sizes.	**Step 2: Plan** Draw a table with three columns and four rows. In the top row, label the columns "Length," "Width," and "Area." In each of the boxes under "Length," write "45 ft." **Step 3: Solve** Chose a number that will give you a product greater than 1,000 but less than 2,000 when multiplied by 45. Combine your strategy with the Guess, Check, and Revise strategy to find the number. 45 ft × 25 ft = 1,125 ft² Write "25 ft" in the box under "Width." Find two other numbers that will give you an area greater than 1,000 ft² but less than 2,000 ft². Multiply to find the areas and then add the areas and dimensions to your table. 45 ft × 35 ft = 1,575 ft² 45 ft × 40 ft = 1,800 ft² **Step 4: Check** Draw a picture with the dimensions labeled to check your work.
Draw a Picture or Use a Model Drawing a picture can help you to understand what you need to solve.	**Step 2: Plan** Draw a rectangle. Label the length "45 ft." **Step 3: Solve** Choose a number that will give you a product greater than 1,000 but less than 2,000 when you multiply it by 45. Combine your strategy with the Guess, Check, and Revise strategy to find the number. Label the width with your number. Find the area of the rectangle. Repeat for two more rectangles. **Step 4: Check** Divide 1,000 by 45. Each width should be greater than the quotient. Divide 2,000 by 45. Each width should be less than the quotient.

Choose a Strategy

YOUR TURN

Choose the Right Word

area   congruent   perimeter

Fill in each blank with the correct word or phrase from the box.

1. The distance around a figure is the _____.

2. The space inside a figure is the _____.

3. If two shapes are exactly the same, then they are _____.

Yes or No?

Answer these questions and be ready to explain your answers.

4. Will increasing one of the dimensions make the area larger? _____

5. Are the perimeter of a figure and the area of a figure the same measurements? _____

6. Does a model need to be the same size as the real object? _____

7. Is the perimeter of a figure measured in square units? _____

Show That You Know

Find the area.

8. rectangle measuring 55 ft × 39 ft

9. rectangle measuring 23 in. × 87 in.

10. rectangle measuring 66 m × 83 m

Which area is greater? Find both areas and circle the one that is greater.

11. 55 m × 14 m or 38 m × 29 m

12. 67 in. × 9 in. or 33 in. × 40 in.

13. 81 ft × 17 ft or 57 ft × 32 ft

READ on Your Own

Reading Comprehension Strategy: Metacognition

Ancient Cultures, *pages 13–14*

VOCABULARY

Watch for the words you are learning about.

excavation: digging to uncover objects hidden in the earth

Fluency Tip

Review any words in boldfaced type before you read. Make sure you know how to pronounce these words.

Before You Read

Think about what you read in "Towers to the Sun." How did the Inca use geometry in their architecture?

As You Read

Read "Artifacts to the Rescue," pages 13–14.

Then write a short description of each kind of excavation below. Include an example of each.

A planned excavation is
_____
_____
_____

A rescue excavation is
_____
_____
_____

An accidental excavation is
_____
_____
_____

After You Read

Describe an artifact you have seen.
_____

Unit 7, Lesson 7   187

Problem Solving

SOLVE on Your Own

Ancient Cultures, *page 15*

Organize the Information

Read You Do the Math in the magazine. Then use the rectangle below to make an area model and show the dimensions of each piece of land.

Area of each piece of land: _____

Area of whole site to be excavated: _____

You Do the Math

Use the information in the area model above to answer these questions. Write your answers in the space provided.

1. How does the area of each piece of land compare to the area of the whole site?

   _____
   _____

> Drawing an area model will help you find the area of each piece of land.

2. Think about an area model when it is filled with unit squares. How is it like an array?

   _____
   _____

After You Solve

What kind of excavation would you like to take part in? Why?

_____
_____
_____

188   Unit 7, Lesson 7

Solve It!

Application

The Four-Step Problem-Solving Plan

Step 1: Read	Step 2: Plan	Step 3: Solve	Step 4: Check
Make sure you understand what the problem is asking.	Decide how you will solve the problem.	Solve the problem using your plan.	Check to make sure your answer is correct.

Read the article below. Then answer the questions.

Javelin Throwing Today

The modern sport of javelin throwing begins when the athlete runs along a runway. Twisting his or her body back, the athlete uses the whole body to throw the javelin overhand as far as possible. The thrower cannot step on or over the scratch line at the end of the runway or the throw is disqualified.

A javelin runway is 4 meters wide and usually 36.5 meters long, although the length of the runway has no limit. About 8 meters from the scratch line is a point in the center of the runway from which the field is measured. Lines are drawn from this center to the left and right edges of the scratch line. The lines make a 29-degree angle. As the lines continue beyond the scratch line, they mark the side-to-side area within which the javelin must land.

1. How would you use an area model to find the area of a javelin runway?

   _____
   _____
   _____
   _____
   _____
   _____
   _____

2. Mr. Warner wants to shorten the javelin runway so that it measures 30 meters long but still measures 4 meters wide. How much greater is the area of the old runway compared to the new runway?

   _____
   _____
   _____

Unit 7, Lesson 8   189

Application
YOUR TURN

Read the article below. Then answer the questions.

The Long Jump

In the long jump of the Ancient Greeks, contestants made five jumps. Each athlete's score was the sum of the lengths of his five jumps. The modern long jump is performed three times by all contestants. Then, the top jumpers move on to the finals. At that point, three more jumps are executed. The jumps are neither averaged nor added up. Instead, the longest of a jumper's six jumps counts as his or her final score.

Jumpers begin by running down a runway that is 45 meters long, although few runners use the entire length of the runway. They run until they hit a takeoff board at the end of the runway and then jump up and out over a landing pit. The landing pit is 10 meters long and filled with sand. The jumper performs a windmill-like motion with his or her legs in the air, and then throws his or her feet forward to land. The jump is measured from the edge of the takeoff board to the nearest mark the jumper's body made in the sand. This is partly why jumpers throw their bodies forward and over their feet as they land.

Fluency Tip
To help you read with expression, pretend you are reading aloud to a friend.

1. Use an area model to find the width of the landing area if its area is 30 m².

   _____

2. What are two important details in the piece?

   _____
   _____
   _____
   _____
   _____
   _____

3. How does making note of the main idea and details as you read help you?

   _____
   _____
   _____
   _____
   _____

190   Unit 7, Lesson 8

Reading Comprehension

READ on Your Own

Reading Comprehension Strategy: Metacognition

Ancient Cultures, pages 16–18

Before You Read

Consider the rescue archaeologists you read about in "Artifacts to the Rescue." What do you think should happen if new builders come across artifacts as they are building?

As You Read

Preview the questions below.

Then read "Ancient Greece," pages 16–18.

Write a brief summary of the passage and then answer the questions.

Summary:
_____
_____
_____

What did you do during each step of reading to help you summarize the article? Give an example for each step.

I identified the topic. Example:
_____

I identified the main idea. Example:
_____
_____

I underlined important details. Example:
_____
_____

After You Read

Why do you think some ancient plays are still performed and studied today?
_____
_____

VOCABULARY

Watch for the words you are learning about.

discus: a heavy disc that is thrown for distance in a track-and-field event

javelin: a thin pole that is thrown for distance in a track-and-field event

mythology: a group or collection of myths and legends

pentathlon: a sporting event made up of five track-and-field events: long jump, discus throw, javelin throw, wrestling, and a 200-yard race

Fluency Tip

Reread sentences that you find difficult. Change your expression as you read.

Unit 7, Lesson 8   191

Problem Solving

SOLVE on Your Own

Ancient Cultures, page 19

Organize the Information

Use the rectangle below to represent the inside of the track. Separate the shape into smaller rectangles and squares to represent each playing area from the Math Project. Make sure you label the dimensions.

Math Project

Use the information in the diagram above to answer the questions below. Write your answers in the space below.

Use your diagram to make a list of the areas of the event spaces.

1. Which of your event spaces had the largest area? Why?

_____

_____

2. How did your diagram help you find the areas for each event?

_____

_____

After You Solve

What could you use the extra space in the middle of the track for?

_____

_____

Unit 7, Lesson 8

Connections

Put It Together

Introducing Using Coordinate Grids to Find Area

You have learned how to name points on the coordinate grid. A coordinate grid is a helpful model to explain area. Remember, area is the number of square units covered by a figure. Look at the coordinate grid below. The rectangle has vertices A (3, 6), B (9, 6), C (9, 2), and D (3, 2).

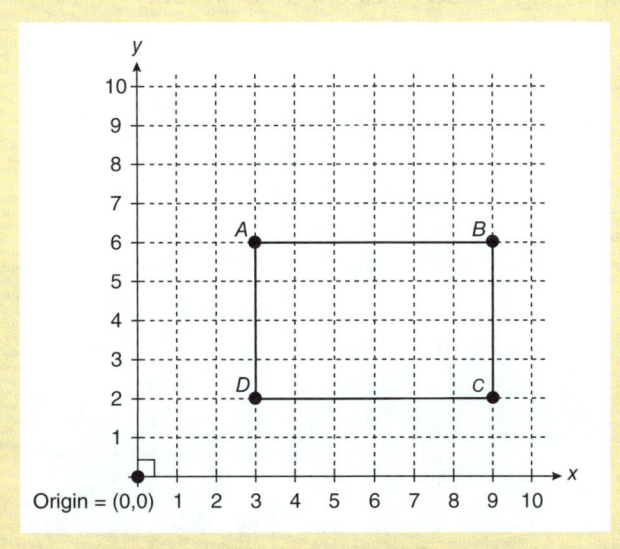

The area of rectangle ABCD can be found by counting the number of squares inside the perimeter. The area has 24 square units.

There is more than one way to find the area. This rectangle has four rows of six columns. The area could be calculated by multiplying $4 \times 6 = 24$ or $6 \times 4 = 24$.

Practicing Using Coordinate Grids to Find Area

Plot the points on a coordinate grid and then count the squares to find the area.

1. A (1, 5), B (5, 5), C (5, 1), and D (1, 1) _____

2. E (0, 4), F (6, 4), G (0, 3) and H (6, 3) _____

3. I (2, 6), J (4, 6), K (4, 1) and L (2, 1) _____

4. M (2, 3), N (5, 3), O (5, 0), and P (2, 0) _____

5. Q (0, 0), R (0, 6), S (8, 6), and T (8, 0) _____

Unit 7, Lesson 9

Connections

YOUR TURN

Thinking About Using Coordinate Grids to Find Area

Think about how you count the number of squares in the coordinate grid to find the area of a rectangle. This method of finding areas by counting squares on the coordinate grid can also be applied to areas that are not rectangular. Consider the polygon with vertices E (2, 7), F (5, 7), G (5, 4), H (7, 4), I (7, 2), J (8, 2), K (8, 1), and I (2, 1). Its eight sides make it an octagon.

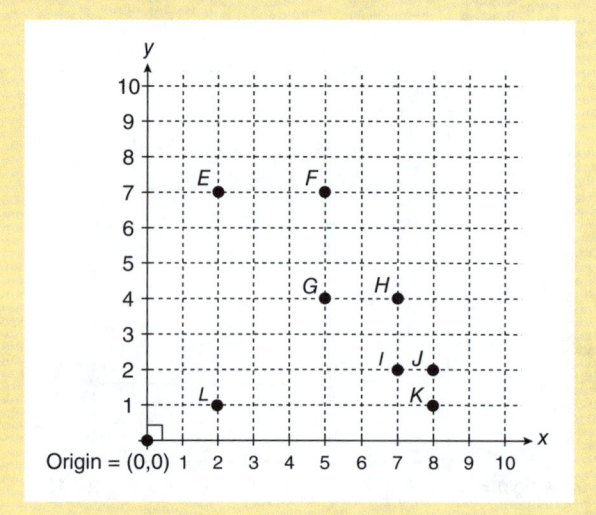

Count the number of square units covered by the figure. The area has 25 square units.

1. Do all figures that have the same area have the same shape? _____

2. What are possible coordinates of a square that has an area of 25 square units?
   _____

3. What are the possible coordinates of a rectangle with an area of 12 square units?
   _____

4. Think about drawing rectangles on a coordinate grid. What are possible dimensions of a rectangle that has an area of 22 square units?
   _____

5. How any different rectangles having an area of 6 square units and a vertex at (0,0) can you draw on a coordinate grid? _____

> **Tip** Once you have plotted the shape, you can either count the grid boxes inside the shape or use a formula to find the area of the shape.

Unit 7, Lesson 9

Show That You Know

Read the information below. Use what you read about using coordinate grids to find areas and answer the questions. Use the space provided to show your work.

> Will learned that archaeologists dig square holes. Once artifacts have been removed from a site they can never be put back exactly as they were found, so archaeologists must record their positions on paper. They use a grid system and measure from a point labeled (0, 0).

You can use grid paper to draw out the foundations described in the problem.

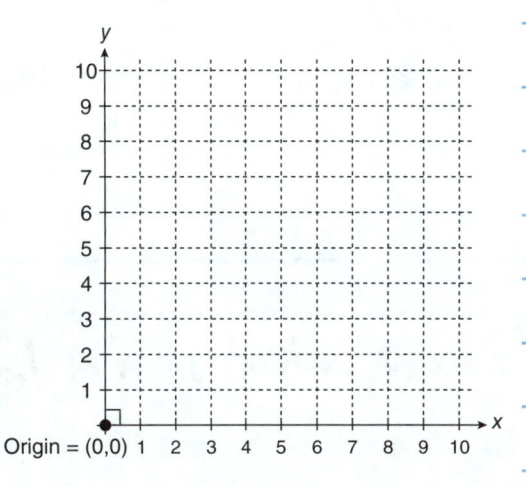

1. A rectangular foundation has been discovered. The corners have coordinates at (2, 2), (2, 5), (7, 2) and (7, 5). What are the length and width of the foundation?

2. What is the area of the foundation?

3. A second rectangular foundation has corners at (5, 8), (8, 8), (8, 3), and (5, 3). What are the length and width of the foundation?

Unit 7, Lesson 9   195

Connections

Show That You Know (continued)

4. What is the area of the foundation?

5. What do you notice about the two foundations?

6. The two rectangles overlap. What is the area of the overlap?

7. What is the total area enclosed by the foundations?

Review What You've Learned

8. What have you learned in this Connections lesson about using coordinate grids?

9. What have you learned in this Connections lesson that you did not already know?

10. How will this lesson help you find the area of other shapes?

Review and Practice

Skills Review

Area

The amount of space taken up by a polygon is the polygon's area.

The standard unit for measuring area is a square that is 1 unit on each side (1 square unit, 1 unit²).

Base and height

One part of a rectangle is the base and another is the height.

Area (A) of a rectangle is found by multiplying the base by the height.

$A = b \times h$

Area units

Area is expressed as square units.

The base and height of a shape can be given in feet (ft), yards (yd), inches (in.) and other measurements.

Area of a square that is 9 in. per side =

9 in. × 9 in. = 81 square inches, or 81 in.²

Area of a rectangle that is 9 ft × 6 ft = 54 ft².

Units of length and width

Length and width may be given in different units. To find area in this case, first convert length or width so that the units match.

A rectangle that is 10 in. × 1 ft =

10 in. × 1 ft is the same as 10 in. × 12 in.

Area of this rectangle = 120 in.²

Strategy Review

- When finding the area of complex shape that is described in writing, first draw a picture of the shape. Then label its dimensions on the drawing. Look for a pattern of simpler shapes within the drawing. Use addition or subtraction of the simple shapes to find the area of the complex shape.

- To make a square or rectangle with a certain area, model the area using unit blocks and determine length and width from the model.
- A table may also be used when making a square or rectangle with a particular area. List length and width values that are factors of the area in the table. Factors may be found by guessing, checking, and revising.

Review and Practice

Skills and Strategies Practice

Complete the exercises below.

1. Find the area of a rectangle that has a base of 3 units and a height of 5 units.

   _____

2. A shape is made of two rectangles. One rectangle is 12 cm × 3 cm and the other is 9 cm × 2 cm. What is the total area of the shape?

   _____

3. Find the area of a rectangle that has a base of 3 in. and a height of 2 ft.

   _____

4. What is the area of a rectangle that is 24 in. × 3 ft?

   _____

5. Find both rectangle areas and determine which is larger.

   A: 25 m × 24 m = _____
   B: 13 m × 31 m = _____

   _____

6. What is the height of a rectangle that has an area of 690 cm² and a base of 69 cm?

   _____

TEST-TAKING tip

When answering a multiple-choice question, first identify the choices you know are wrong. For example, a test question may ask you to find the area of a rectangle that is 5 in. by 13 in. The answer choices are 50 in.², 40 in.², 55 in.², and 65 in.² You may not know the answer to 5 × 13 off the top of your head, but you probably know that it is not 50, because 5 × 10 = 50, and it is not 40, because 5 × 8 = 40.

Mid-Unit Review

Circle the letter of the correct answer.

1. The area of a rectangle that has a base of 9 units and a height of 7 units is _____.

   A. 16 square units C. 63 square units
   B. 2 square units   D. 54 square units

2. What is the area of a 2 ft × 1 yd rectangle?

   A. 2 ft²   B. 6 ft²   C. 1 ft²   D. 9 ft²

3. What is the area of a rectangular board that has a base of 5 units and a height of 6 units?

   A. 6 square units   C. 11 square units
   B. 25 square units D. 30 square units

4. A backyard measures 50 m × 10 m. What is its area?

   A. 5 m²   B. 50 m²   C. 0.5 m²   D. 500 m²

5. A square is 4 units on each side. What is its area?

   A. 16 units²   C. 4 units²
   B. 12 units²   D. 24 units²

6. A square is 4 cm². What is the length of its side?

   A. 2 cm   B. 1 cm   C. 4 cm   D. 8 cm

7. What is the area of a rectangle that is 3 units long and 20 units high?

   A. 6 units²   C. 23 units²
   B. 60 units²   D. 17 units²

8. How many feet are there in 1 yard?

   A. 3   B. 2   C. 12   D. $\frac{1}{3}$

9. A 25 m² rectangle has a 25 m base. What is its height?

   A. 5 m   B. 2 m   C. 1 m   D. 1.5 m

10. What is the area of a rectangle that is 9 × 10 units?

    A. 19 square units
    B. 90 square units
    C. 27 square units
    D. 81 square units

11. There are _____ inches in 1 foot.

    A. 6   B. 10   C. 8   D. 12

12. A 24 cm² rectangle has a height of 12 cm. Its base is _____ cm.

    A. 10   B. 22   C. 12   D. 2

13. What is the area of a rectangle that is 8 cm × 8 cm?

    A. 64 cm²
    B. 64 cm
    C. 16 cm²
    D. 56 cm

Unit 7, Lesson 10

Review and Practice

Mid-Unit Review

14. What is the area of a piece of paper that has a base of 2 units and a height of 10 units?

A. 24 square units
B. 10 square units
C. 6 square units
D. 20 square units

15. What is the area of a 4 in. × 2 ft rectangle?

A. 8 in.² B. 48 in.² C. 96 in.² D. 40 in.²

16. What is the height of a rectangle with a base of 7 units and an area of 84 units?

A. 14 units
B. 12 units
C. 13 units
D. 10 units

17. A 100 in.² rectangle has a 25 in. base. What is its height?

A. 2 in. B. 4 in. C. 50 in. D. 75 in.

18. What is the area of a rectangular sign that is 7 units wide and 8 units high?

A. 15 units²   C. 16 units²
B. 49 units²   D. 56 units²

19. A 60 m² rectangle has a 5 m base. What is its height?

A. 10 m B. 11 m C. 12 m D. 13 m

20. What is the area of a 3 ft by 5 yd rectangle?

A. 45 square feet   C. 45 feet
B. 15 square feet   D. 8 square feet

21. A 49 cm² rectangle has a height of 7 cm. Its base is _____ cm.

A. 7   B. 8   C. 343   D. 42

22. A square is 1 mile on each side. What is its area?

A. 1 mile   C. 1 square mile
B. 2 miles   D. 2 square miles

23. What is the area of a 1 in. × 1 ft rectangle?

A. 12 in.   C. 10 in.²
B. 12 in.²   D. 6 in.²

24. A rectangle has a height of 3 inches and a base of 11 inches. What is its area?

A. 33 in.   C. 30 in.
B. 33 in.²   D. 30 in.²

25. The area of a rectangle that has a base of 9 units and a height of 11 units is _____.

A. 99 square units   C. 20 square units
B. 90 square units   D. 2 square units

Estimating Area

Learn the SKILL

Charlene is looking at a right triangle. The base of the triangle is 3 units in length and the height is 4 units. How can Charlene estimate the area of the triangle?

VOCABULARY

Watch for the words you are learning about.

partial unit: a part of a whole unit
superimpose: to lay or place on top of something else

SKILL	EXAMPLE	COMPLETE THE EXAMPLE
As you learned earlier, the area of a figure is the number of square units the figure encloses.	Find the area of a rectangle that has a base of 4 units and a height of 6 units. 4 units × 6 units = 24 square units	Find the area of a square that has a side of 8 units. _____
If there is a figure other than a square or rectangle, it is possible to **superimpose** a grid of square units over it. Notice that some of the squares are not complete. Using smaller unit squares can give a better estimate of the area.	Superimpose a grid on the figure of a right triangle with a base of 3 units and a height of 4 units. height = 4 units base = 3 units	Superimpose a grid on the figure of a right triangle with a base of 6 units and a height of 8 units.
You can count the square units to estimate the area. Some of the units are **partial units.** You can estimate to round the units to either 1 whole, $\frac{1}{2}$, or 0.	Estimate the area of a right triangle with a base of 3 units and a height of 4 units. Count the number of unit square that cover the triangle. About 5 whole square units and 2 half unit squares are counted. The total area is estimated as $5 + \frac{1}{2} + \frac{1}{2}$ or 6 square units.	Estimate the area of a right triangle with a base of 6 units and height of 8 units. _____

Unit 7, Lesson 11

Learn the Skill

YOUR TURN

Choose the Right Word

> area   estimate   partial unit   unit

Fill in each blank with the correct word or phrase from the box.

1. A(n) _____ is an answer that is close to the correct answer.

2. A(n) _____ is part of a whole unit.

3. The number of square units a figure encloses is its _____.

4. A(n) _____ is a part into which a whole can be analyzed.

Yes or No?

Answer these questions and be ready to explain your answers.

5. Would less than one half of a unit be counted as one? _____

6. Would more than half of a unit be counted as one? _____

7. Can a grid of square units be superimposed on any figure? _____

8. Would a grid with smaller unit squares give a better estimate? _____

Show That You Know

Estimate the area of each figure.

9.   2 units / 4 units

10.   3 units / 5 units

Unit 7, Lesson 11

SOLVE on Your Own

Learn the Skill

Skills Practice

Okay, now you know all about estimating area. Show it by completing these exercises.

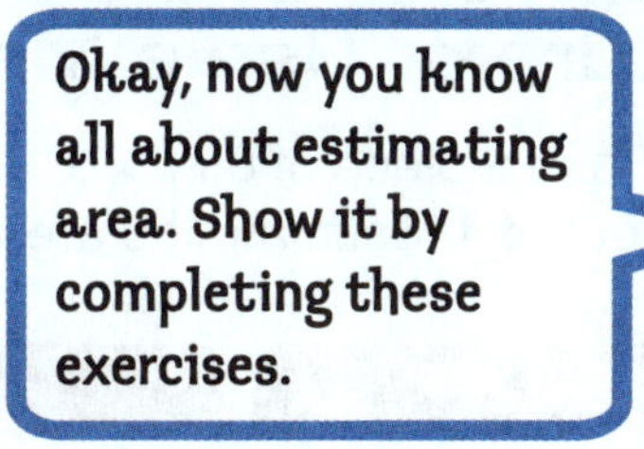

Estimate the area of each figure. Write your answer on the line.

1.

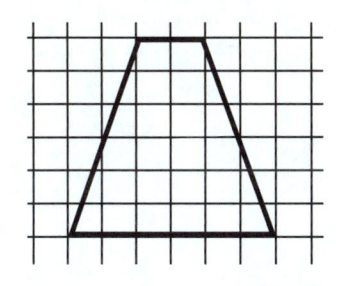

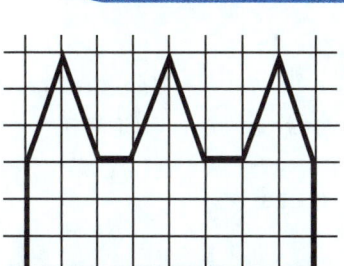

2.

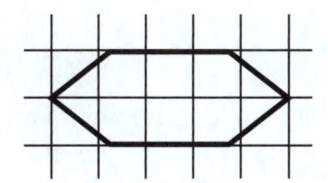

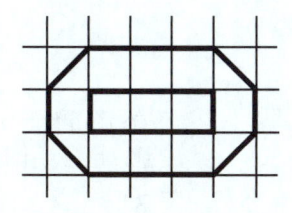

3.

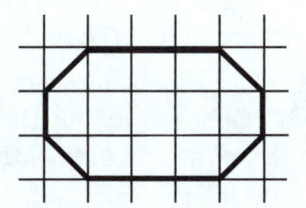

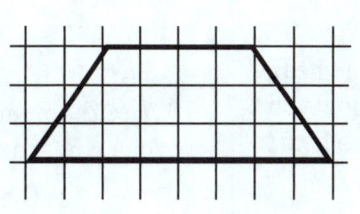

4.

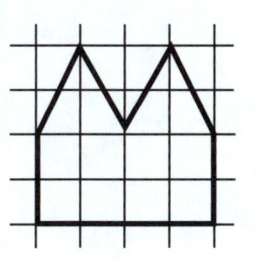

5.

6.

7.

8.

Unit 7, Lesson 11   203

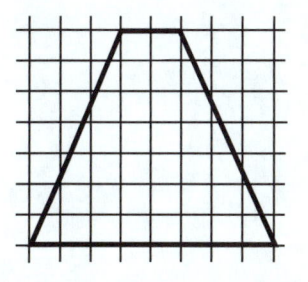

Choose a Strategy

Estimating Area

Strategies

**Try a Simpler Form of the Problem,
Draw a Picture or Use a Model**

Step 1: Read Take a piece of 8 in. × 11 in. paper and cut a heart shape out of it. Estimate the area of the heart.

STRATEGY	SOLUTION
Try a Simpler Form of the Problem A heart is similar in shape to a triangle. You can estimate the area by using the steps to find the area for a triangle.	**Step 2: Plan** Measure width of the triangle at its widest point. Measure the length of the triangle from the point at the bottom to the line at its top. **Step 3: Solve** *(diagram of heart showing width across the top and length from top to bottom point)* To find the area of a triangle, you multiply the length × width and divide the answer by 2. 8 in. × 11 in. = 88 in.² 88 in.² ÷ 2 = 44 in.² **Step 4: Check** Draw unit squares inside the heart. How many can you fit inside? How many half-squares did you draw?
Draw a Picture or Use a Model Drawing a picture of the heart on graph paper will allow you to estimate the area of the heart.	**Step 2: Plan** Trace your heart on a piece of graph paper that has unit squares. Add the area of each unit square to find the total area. **Step 3: Solve** Count the number of squares in each row of your heart. Write the number of squares to the side of the heart. Add up the numbers when you are done. This number will be the estimated area of the heart. **Step 4: Check** Instead of counting the number of squares in each row, count the number of squares in each column.

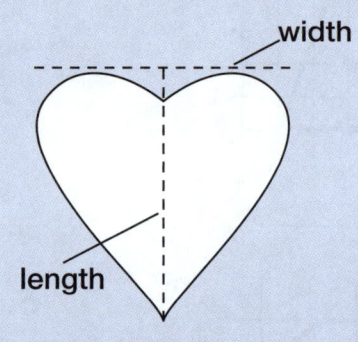

YOUR TURN

Choose the Right Word

> area   estimate   unit square

Fill in each blank with the correct word or phrase from the box.

1. You find the _____ of a rectangle by multiplying its length by its width.

2. A(n) _____ has the dimensions of 1 unit × 1 unit.

3. If you want to find the area of an irregular shape, you might _____ to find the area.

Choose a Strategy

Yes or No?

Answer these questions and be ready to explain your answers.

4. Sara drew a star on a piece of paper. Will the area of her shape be larger than the area of the paper? _____

5. When you estimate, do you get an exact answer? _____

6. Is area always given in square units? _____

7. Will the area of a triangle be larger than the area of a rectangle if their height and width are the same? _____

Show That You Know

Estimate the answer to each problem. Round the numbers to the nearest 10.

8. 40.5 in. × 50.2 in.

9. 28 m × 61.3 m

10. 72.2 ft × 13 ft

Find the area of each rectangle. Do not estimate.

11. 38 cm × 45 cm

12. 112 m × 44 m

13. 25 in. × 25 in.

Unit 7, Lesson 12   205

Reading Comprehension

READ on Your Own

Reading Comprehension Strategy: Metacognition

Ancient Cultures, pages 20–21

Fluency Tip
Review any words in boldfaced type before you read. Make sure you know how to pronounce these words.

Before You Read

In "Ancient Greece," you learned about different people who were important to the Greeks. Who are some people you admire in our society?

As You Read

Read "Your Land or Your Life!", pages 20–21.

Then complete the sequence chart below. Read the description of each event. Number each event in the order in which it occurs in the reading.

Events in the Life of Alexander the Great	Order of Events
Alexander tamed a horse that no one else had been able to ride.	
Alexander was taught by the famous philosopher, Aristotle.	
Alexander's father died and Alexander became king.	
Alexander conquered Persia.	

After You Read

Alexander wanted to control the world, and he became very greedy. How has wanting something affected you?

_____

_____

Problem Solving

SOLVE on Your Own

Ancient Cultures, *page 22*

Organize the Information

Read You Do the Math in the magazine. Then fill in the table below with information about each rectangle you draw.

Shape	Length on Map	Width on Map	Area on Map
Rectangle 1			
Rectangle 2			
Rectangle 3			
Rectangle 4			
Rectangle 5			
Rectangle 6			

Total Area: _____

You Do the Math

Use the information in the table above to answer these questions. Write your answers in the space provided.

Think about how estimating is different from finding exact numbers.

1. You found the area of the land shown on the map in square centimeters. How could you use your measurements to find the area in square kilometers?

   _____
   _____

2. How accurate are your measurements? Why?

   _____
   _____

After You Solve

Alexander was a king. What are some other names for rulers of a country?

_____

Unit 7, Lesson 12

Learn the Skill

Decomposing Shapes to Find Area

Learn the SKILL

VOCABULARY
Watch for the words you are learning about.
formula: symbols that make a mathematical statement

Margaret is looking at a right triangle. The base of the triangle is 8 units and the height is 6 units. How can Margaret find the area of the triangle using a formula?

SKILL	EXAMPLE	WRITE AN EXAMPLE
The area of a rectangle can be described by a **formula**, which is a mathematical statement using symbols. For example, b is base and h is height.	Find the area of a rectangle with a base of 3 units and a height of 4 units. $A = b \times h$ $A = 3 \times 4$ $A = 12$ square units	Pick dimensions for a square. _____ Find the area. _____
A rectangle can be decomposed into two congruent triangles. The area of each triangle is half the area of the rectangle. The area of a triangle is $A = \frac{1}{2} \times$ base $\times$ height or $A = \frac{1}{2}b \times h$.	Find the area of a triangle with a base of 10 units and a height of 6 units. $A = \frac{1}{2} \times$ base $\times$ height $A = \frac{1}{2} \times 10$ units $\times 6$ units $A = 30$ square units Multiplying by $\frac{1}{2}$ is the same as dividing by 2.	Pick a base and height for a triangle. base = _____ units height = _____ units Find the area. _____
You have also learned to decompose other polygons. Use the decomposed shapes and the formulas for the area of rectangles and triangles to find the area of a polygon.	Find the area of the shape below. 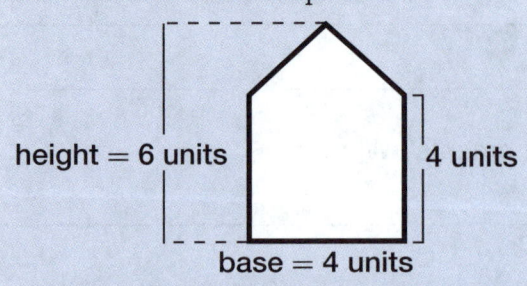 height = 6 units, 4 units, base = 4 units The pentagon is decomposed into a 4 × 4 square and a 4 × 2 triangle. The area is: $A = (4 \text{ units} \times 4 \text{ units}) +$ $(\frac{1}{2} \times 4 \text{ units} \times 2 \text{ units})$ $= 16$ square units $+ 4$ square units $= 20$ square units	Find the area of the shape below. 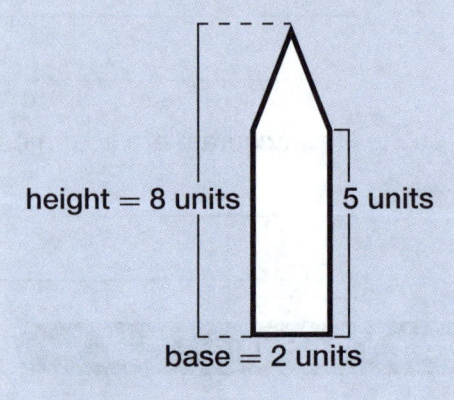 height = 8 units, 5 units, base = 2 units

Unit 7, Lesson 13

YOUR TURN

Choose the Right Word

decomposed   polygon   triangle

Fill in each blank with the correct word or phrase from the box.

1. A figure can be _____ into other shapes.

2. A _____ is a figure with three or more line segments that connect but do not cross.

3. A _____ is a polygon with three sides.

Learn the Skill

Yes or No?

Answer these questions and be ready to explain your answers.

4. Can a square be decomposed into two triangles? _____

5. Can a pentagon be decomposed into squares? _____

6. Can an octagon be decomposed into triangles? _____

7. Can all polygons be decomposed into smaller shapes? _____

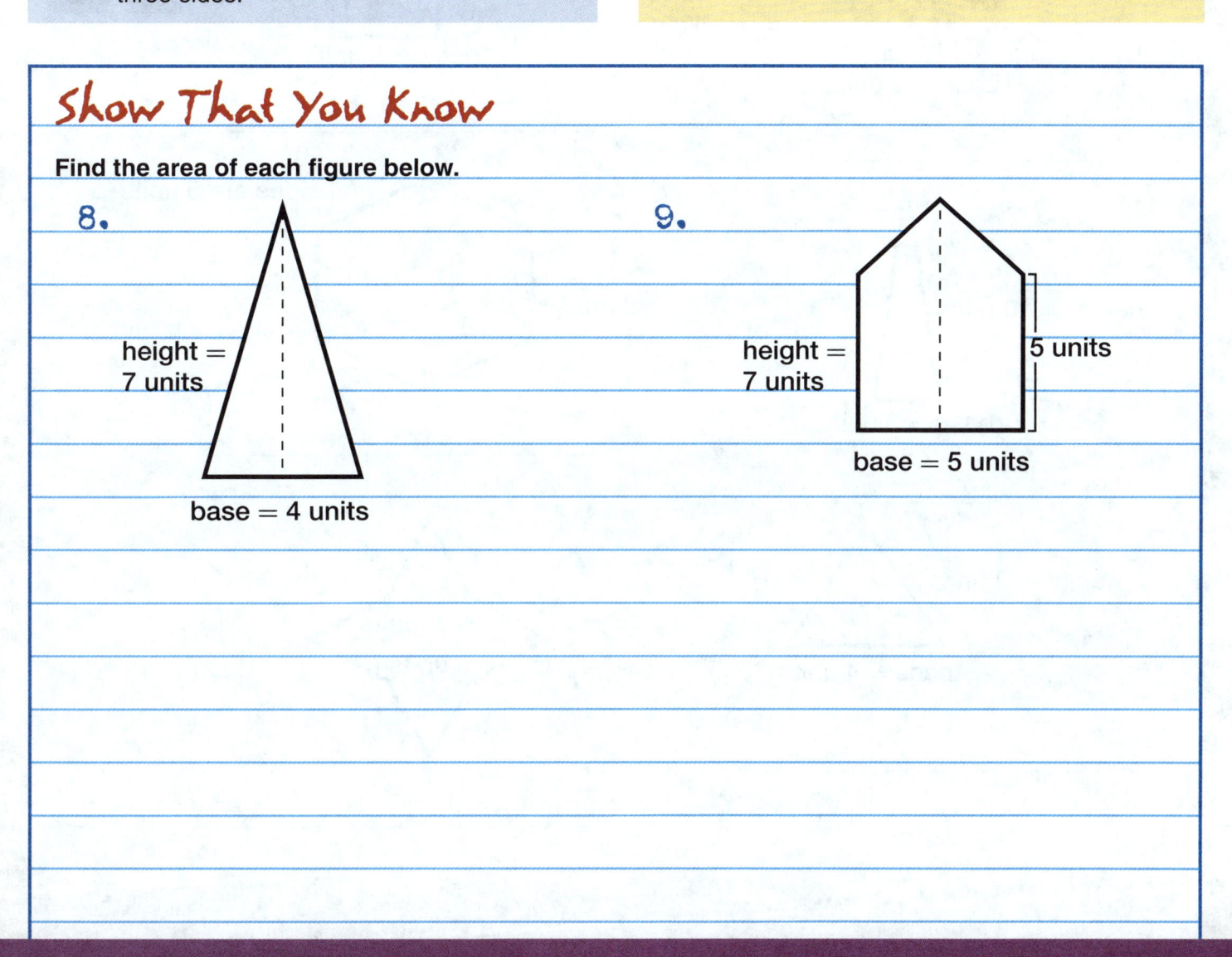

Show That You Know

Find the area of each figure below.

8. height = 7 units, base = 4 units

9. height = 7 units, base = 5 units, 5 units

Unit 7, Lesson 13   209

Learn the Skill

SOLVE on Your Own

Skills Practice

Find the area of each figure. Write the area on the line.

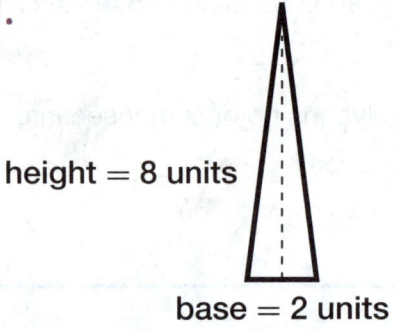

Remember to divide by 2 when you find the area of a triangle.

1. height = 8 units, base = 2 units

2. height = 10 units, base = 3 units

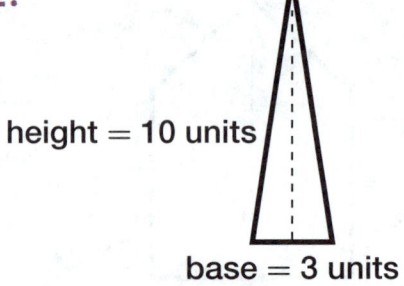

3. height = 3 units, base = 4 units

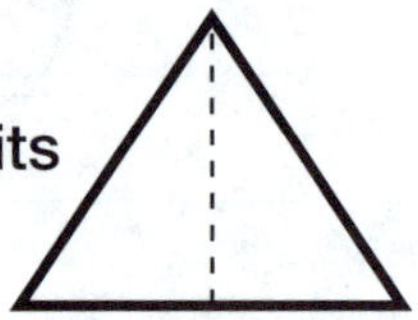

4. height = 7 units, 3 units, base = 3 units

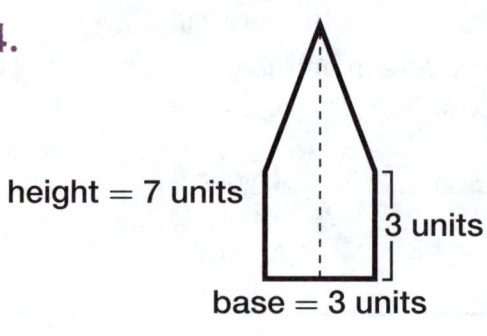

5. All sides are 5 units, 11 units, 8 units

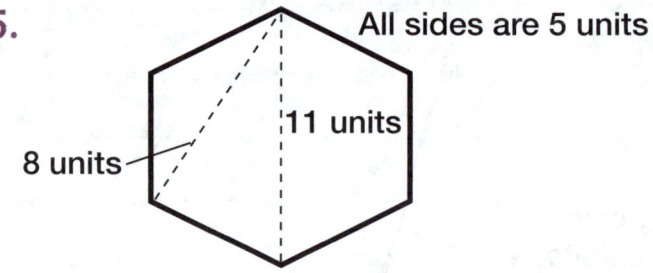

6. 6 units, 6 units

210   Unit 7, Lesson 13

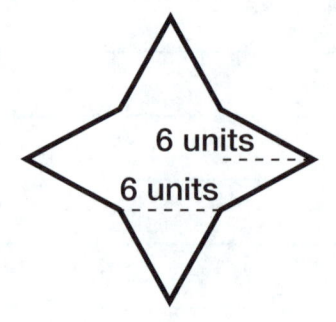

Choose a Strategy

Decomposing Shapes to Find Area

Strategies
Draw a Picture or Use a Model,
Try a Simpler Form of the Problem

Step 1: Read Jamal and Pam are making scenery for a play. They cut seven triangular mountains from cardboard, each with a height of 11 feet and a base of 8 feet. They have 1 gallon of paint, which will cover 400 square feet. Is this enough paint to cover all seven mountains?

STRATEGY	SOLUTION
Draw a Picture or Use a Model Drawing a picture of the shape will help you to see how to solve the problem.	**Step 2: Plan** Draw a triangle. Label the base 8 feet and the height 11 feet. Use these measurements to find the total area of one triangle, and then multiply it by 7. **Step 3: Solve** Find the area of a rectangle by multiplying the height × base. A triangle is half of a rectangle, so you can find the area of a triangle by multiplying the height × base and dividing the answer by 2. 11 ft × 8 ft = 88 ft² 88 ft² ÷ 2 = 44 ft² Since there are seven mountains, multiply the answer by 7 to find out the total area. 44 ft² × 7 = 308 ft² There will be enough paint. **Step 4: Check** You can work backward to check. 308 ÷ 7 = 44 44 × 2 = 88 88 ÷ 8 = 11 The answer checks.
Try a Simpler Form of the Problem When you have a new type of problem, it is helpful to use skills learned before to help to solve the problem.	**Step 2: Plan** Decompose a triangle into a rectangle. Then multiply to find the total area. **Step 3: Solve** Draw dotted lines to make a rectangle. If you cut the triangle in half and move the other half, you would have a rectangle. The base of this rectangle is half the width of the triangle you started with. Multiply base × height. 4 ft × 11 ft = 44 ft² 44 ft² × 7 = 308 ft² There will be enough paint. **Step 4: Check** Use a grid to check if your answer is reasonable.

height = 11 ft

base = 8 ft

Unit 7, Lesson 14

Choose a Strategy

YOUR TURN

Choose the Right Word

> base   dimensions   height

Fill in each blank with the correct word or phrase from the box.

1. The _____ of a figure is how tall it is.

2. When you measure the height of a triangle, you measure from the _____ to the tip.

3. To find the area of a square, you multiply its _____.

Yes or No?

Answer these questions and be ready to explain your answers.

4. If you multiply the base × height, will you have the area of a triangle? _____

5. If one dimension of a figure is increased, will the area increase? _____

6. Will every problem-solving strategy work for every math problem? _____

7. To find the height of a triangle, should you measure one of the sides? _____

Show That You Know

Use what you know about triangles to answer the questions below.

8. Four triangles each have bases that measure 15 inches and heights that measure 12 inches. What is the combined area of the four triangles?

9. Which triangle has a larger area?
   Triangle 1—80 in. × 22 in.
   Triangle 2—60 in. × 33 in.

Find the area of each triangle. Show your work.

10. 10 ft × 76 ft

11. 99 in. × 36 in.

12. 61 m × 18 m

13. 5 yd × 62 yd

212   Unit 7, Lesson 14

Reading Comprehension

READ on Your Own

Reading Comprehension Strategy: Metacognition

Ancient Cultures, pages 23–24

Fluency Tip
Review any words in boldfaced type before you read. Make sure you know how to pronounce these words.

Before You Read

In "Your Land or Your Life!", you learned that Alexander named a town for himself. He called it Alexandria. What places do you know that were named for famous people?

As You Read

Read "Not Just the Egyptians," pages 23–24.

Then read the descriptions of different pyramids below. On the line, write the name of the culture that built that kind of pyramid.

Pyramid Description	Culture
These pyramids were made of stone blocks. They were tall and thin, so they rose very steeply.	_____
These pyramids were made of different-sized rectangles placed on top of each other. They were used for worship.	_____
These pyramids were mounds of clay with flat tops. Some were made of stone plates.	_____
These pyramids were made of stone and were wider than they were tall. They were covered with symbols.	_____

After You Read

What are some ways that people decorate graves today?

_____

_____

Problem Solving

SOLVE on Your Own

Ancient Cultures, page 25

Organize the Information

Read You Do the Math in the magazine. Then fill in the table below with information about the dimensions of your model.

Side	Width	Height	Area
square base			
triangular faces			

Total Area: _____

You Do the Math

Use the information in the table above to answer these questions. Write your answers in the space provided.

1. What are some possible dimensions of a rectangle with the same total area as your model?

   _____
   _____

2. If you bought a sheet of cardboard that was a meter on each side, would you have enough material to make your model?

   _____
   _____
   _____

> Remember to include all of the sides of the pyramid in the total area.

After You Solve

Some cultures are remembered for their huge pyramids. What do people do today to make sure that they are remembered?

_____
_____

214   Unit 7, Lesson 14

Solve It!

Application

The Four-Step Problem-Solving Plan

Step 1: Read	Step 2: Plan	Step 3: Solve	Step 4: Check
Make sure you understand what the problem is asking.	Decide how you will solve the problem.	Solve the problem using your plan.	Check to make sure your answer is correct.

Read the article below. Then answer the questions.

Stupas: Sacred Buildings

Buddhism is a religion that began in India over 2,500 years ago. Over time, Buddhism spread east into Asia and Southeast Asia. In India, Buddhists (followers of Buddhism) built sacred shrines called *stupas* to house artifacts. They were originally built at sites that related to Buddha, the religion's founder, during his life. Later, stupas were built all throughout India and Asia.

Stupas are small, domed-shaped structures with gates facing each of the four major directions. Followers visit them and walk around the outside of the stupa in a clockwise direction. The building itself is believed to be as important as the item or items inside.

A stupa is often large enough to walk into, in which case there is usually a statue within. But there are also very small stupas that are just a little more than a few yards across. These were often built close to places of worship. Followers look after the stupa and the surrounding grounds.

1. How might you estimate the area of a round stupa?

   _____
   _____
   _____
   _____
   _____
   _____

2. What do you think was the author's purpose in writing the article?

   _____
   _____
   _____
   _____
   _____
   _____

Unit 7, Lesson 15   215

Application

YOUR TURN

Read the article below. Then answer the questions.

Pagodas

As Buddhism spread east, the small stupas took on new shapes. In Sri Lanka, the buildings looked bell-shaped. In China, Korea, and Japan, the structures were called *pagodas*. They were square, polygonal, or circular, and multi-storied, with many levels of roofs. Like stupas, they were often small buildings that housed texts and scrolls rather than people.

Asian pagodas can be very tall. They are made of a pattern of repeating stories in regularly decreasing measurements. Each story has its own projecting roofline, which may be very decorative. A pagoda is mostly meant to be a monument. It often has very little space inside.

Originally, pagodas were the center and focus of an Asian temple. After a while, they became less important and were moved away from the center to the side. Sometimes, they were even moved outside the grounds of the temple completely.

Fluency Tip
If you find yourself reading so quickly that you are missing the meaning, slow down.

1. What purpose did you set for yourself before you began to read?
   _____
   _____

2. What were two details you noticed in the reading?
   _____
   _____
   _____
   _____

3. How might estimate the area of a section of pagoda roof?
   _____
   _____
   _____
   _____

Reading Comprehension

READ on Your Own

Reading Comprehension Strategy: Metacognition

Ancient Cultures, pages 26–28

Fluency Tip
Everyone reads at a different pace. Practice until you can read at a pace that is comfortable for you.

Before You Read

Consider the different kinds of pyramids you read about in "Not Just the Egyptians." What kinds of houses do you think were common in these cultures? Why?

As You Read

Read "Building an Empire," pages 26–28. 🛑

What did you do to identify the text structure of the pages?

_____
_____

What features helped you identify the text structure?

_____

What kind of graphic organizer could you use to organize the information?

_____

Why is thinking about the text structure of a passage and using a graphic organizer helpful?

_____
_____

After You Read

What different types of homes have you seen before?

_____
_____
_____

Unit 7, Lesson 15   217

Problem Solving

SOLVE on Your Own

Ancient Cultures, page 29

Organize the Information

Use the table below to organize the information in the Math Project in the magazine. Use the scale given on page 29 to write your dimensions in inches, not feet.

Surface	Dimensions	Area	Number of Surfaces	Total Area of Surfaces
1st story wall			4	
2nd story wall			4	
3rd story wall			4	
1st story roof			1	
2nd story roof			1	
3rd story roof			1	

Total Area: _____

Math Project

Use the information in the table above to answer these questions. Write your answers in the space provided.

1. How did you use the scale to find the dimensions for your model?

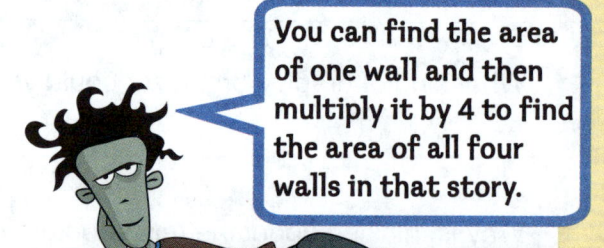

   _____
   _____

> You can find the area of one wall and then multiply it by 4 to find the area of all four walls in that story.

2. Cardboard is sold by the square foot, so the total amount of cardboard needed will have to be rounded. Would it be better to round up or down? Explain your answer.

   _____

After You Solve

Why do you think people build models?

_____
_____

Unit 7, Lesson 15

Using Symmetry and Congruence to Understand Transformations

Learn the SKILL

VOCABULARY

Watch for the words you are learning about.

rotational symmetry: rotation that shows congruence

tessellation: when one or more shapes is repeated, fitting together without any overlap or gaps

tiling: another word for tessellation

Sara wants to create new wallpaper for her room. She knows she wants to completely cover the wall using triangles. How can she arrange the triangles so there are no overlaps or gaps in her design?

SKILL	EXAMPLE	WRITE AN EXAMPLE
As you learned in Unit 6, transformations can be translations (slides), rotations (turns), or reflections (flips). The figures are congruent.	How has the figure been transformed? The figure is translated down and right and rotated to the right.	Describe the steps used to transform triangle 1 to create triangle 2. 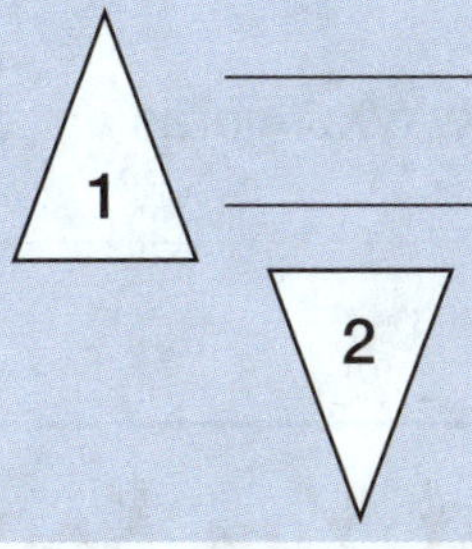
A reflection or flip can be done over a line of symmetry. In **rotational symmetry,** one figure is rotated to show that it is congruent to another figure or itself.	Identify the type of symmetry. 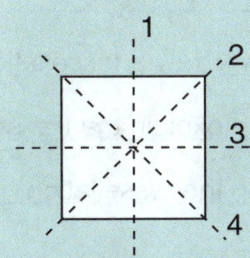 A square has rotational symmetry and four lines of symmetry.	Draw a triangle with a line of symmetry but no rotational symmetry.
A **tessellation** or **tiling** is formed by repeating one shape over and over again without any overlap or gaps. A tessellation can be drawn by using translations, rotations, and flips.	Draw a tessellation of triangles. 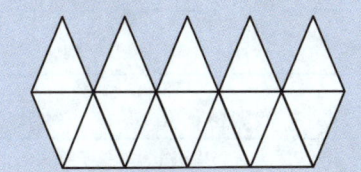	Draw a tessellation using rectangles.

Learn the Skill

YOUR TURN

Choose the Right Word

> rotational symmetry   tessellation   tiling
> transformation

Fill in each blank with the correct word or phrase from the box.

1. Making a tessellation is the same as making a _____.

2. A _____ is a change in the position or direction of a figure.

3. A _____ created when a shape is repeated without any overlap or gaps.

4. You can show two figures are congruent using _____.

Yes or No?

Answer these questions and be ready to explain your answers.

5. Is it possible to draw a tessellation in which the only shape is a circle? _____

6. Are translated figures congruent? _____

7. Do two triangles formed by a diagonal of a rectangle have rotational symmetry? _____

8. Does rotational symmetry create a mirror image? _____

Show That You Know

Complete the exercises below.

9. What transformations can be used to show that these two triangles are congruent? What kind of symmetry does this show for the square?

   [square divided by a diagonal into triangle 1 and triangle 2]

10. Draw a tessellation of a rectangle and explain the transformations needed to make the tessellation.

220   Unit 7, Lesson 16

Learn the Skill

SOLVE on Your Own

Skills Practice

Tell whether the figures are congruent or not. If the figures are congruent, name the transformations that can be used to show they are congruent.

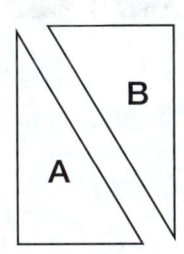

Remember that a figure may have more than one type of symmetry.

Draw a tessellation using the given shape. If the tessellation is not possible, write "Not possible."

1.

2.

3.

4. squares

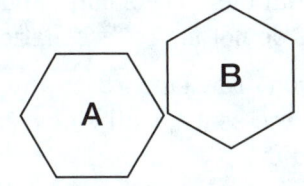

5. circles

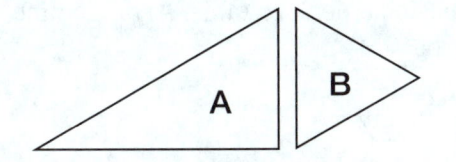

6. hexagons

Unit 7, Lesson 16   221

Choose a Strategy

Using Symmetry and Congruence to Understand Transformations

Strategy
Draw a Picture or Use a Model

Step 1: Read Brittany and Kim are building a table. They want to cover the top of the table with the same shape. They need the shapes to touch and to cover the entire table top in a tessellation. They have four shapes to choose from: stars, squares, hexagons, or circles. Which shapes would work for their table?

STRATEGY	SOLUTION
Draw a Picture or Use a Model Drawing pictures of the shapes and seeing how they fit together will allow you to solve the problem.	**Step 2: Plan** Choose one of the shapes. Draw it on your paper. **Step 3: Solve** Draw a row of three of the shapes touching each other. Draw two rows of three under the first row. Do the shapes touch each other and leave no extra space? Circles do not, so they do not make a tessellation. Which of the other shapes make tessellations? The square and hexagon make tessellations. The star and circle do not make tessellations. **Step 4: Check** Color the shapes you drew blue. Color any extra space between the shapes in red. If you have red space, your shapes do not make a tessellation.
Draw a Picture or Use a Model Using a model can help you to understand how shapes fit together and if they make a tessellation.	**Step 2: Plan** Cut out nine copies of each shape. Be careful to make all the shapes the same size. **Step 3: Solve** Lay the shapes on a desk or table. Arrange nine hexagons together in rows of three. They fit together without any of the table showing through. So they make a tessellation. **Step 4: Check** Try to move the shapes around by turning them to see if you can make them fit together more closely.

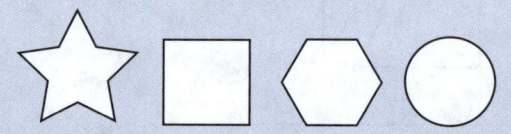

Unit 7, Lesson 17

YOUR TURN

Choose the Right Word

> square   tessellation   triangles

Fill in each blank with the correct word or phrase from the box.

1. A repeating pattern of shapes with no extra area between the shapes is a _____.

2. A _____ can be used to make a tessellation.

3. Some _____ can be used to make tessellations, but others cannot.

Choose a Strategy

Yes or No?

Answer these questions and be ready to explain your answers.

4. If a pattern repeats, is it always a tessellation? _____

5. If you place them in rows, can squares form a tessellation? _____

6. Is a pentagon is a six-sided shape? _____

7. Is an array the same as a tessellation? _____

Show That You Know

Which of these are tessellations? Explain your answer.

8.

9.

Can you tell if this shape will make a tessellation? Explain how you can tell.

10.

11.

12.

Unit 7, Lesson 17   223

Reading Comprehension

READ on Your Own

Reading Comprehension Strategy: Metacognition

Ancient Cultures, pages 30–31

VOCABULARY

Watch for the words you are learning about.

arch: a curved structure used to support a building or bridge

mosaics: designs made with many small tiles

Fluency Tip

Review any words in boldfaced type before you read. Make sure you know how to pronounce these words.

Before You Read

What building materials are used to make houses today? Does where a person lives tell us anything about the person?

As You Read

Read "In the Eyes of the Beholder," pages 30–31. STOP

Then read the statements in the left column. In the middle column, write a T if it is true and an F if it is false. In the right column, rewrite the false statements so that they are true.

Statement	True or False?	Correct Statement
The cave paintings in Chauvet, France, were painted 300 years ago.		
Egyptian pyramids were built as graves for their leaders.		
Greeks often painted scenes from mythology to decorate their pots.		
The Dome of the Rock is an ancient Greek building.		

After You Read

What is done with special artworks in your culture?

_____

_____

Problem Solving

SOLVE on Your Own

Ancient Cultures, page 32

Organize the Information

Read You Do the Math in the magazine. Then use the photograph to find tessellations. List some facts about tessellations on the lines below.

_____
_____
_____
_____

You Do the Math

Use the information in the list above to answer these questions. Write your answers in the space provided.

> Listing facts about tessellations will help you find them in the photograph.

1. Can more than one shape be used in a tessellation?
_____
_____

2. Are circles polygons? Does this make it easier or harder for them to make tessellations? Explain your answer.
_____
_____

3. What are some ways you can tell a shape will not make a tessellation even if you do not draw it or use a model?
_____

After You Solve

Where have you seen tessellations?
_____
_____

Unit 7, Lesson 17

Application

Solve It!

The Four-Step Problem-Solving Plan

Step 1: Read	Step 2: Plan	Step 3: Solve	Step 4: Check
Make sure you understand what the problem is asking.	Decide how you will solve the problem.	Solve the problem using your plan.	Check to make sure your answer is correct.

Read the article below. Then answer the questions.

Modern Symbols

The modern world is full of symbols. Think about the symbols of modern language, such as Chinese characters, Arabic letters, and the English alphabet. However, there are many other symbols that go beyond languages. These symbols can help people traveling in a foreign country. They can also help people who have difficulty reading or seeing words. For example, a picture may show falling rocks on a bright yellow diamond-shaped sign. This communicates that you might not want to drive too close to the rock walls of a canyon. Similarly, a bright white H on a deep blue background symbolizes "hospital" in many countries. A red plus sign on a white background means "first aid." What does this symbol mean to you?

How is that different from this one?

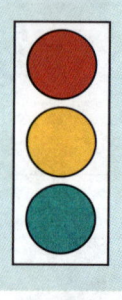

1. Think about the symbols around you. Are there any in your classroom or a nearby hallway? Draw one and tell what it means.

   _____
   _____

2. What are some common symbols you see around you everyday?

   _____
   _____
   _____
   _____

226 Unit 7, Lesson 18

YOUR TURN

Application

Read the article below. Then answer the questions.

What Does That Mean?

You use symbols all the time and often never stop to think about it. If you study a musical instrument, you have been learning another entire language of symbols. Quick, how many ♩ do you need to equal one of these: 𝅗𝅥 ? Even if you do not play an instrument, you may know the answer is two.

When home computers became common, so did e-mail and instant messaging. Both e-mail and instant messaging use a shorter, more casual style of writing for communication. Often, however, it is hard to tell how a piece of writing was intended. Was the writer making a joke or being serious? Should the reader laugh or be offended? Emoticons, such as the smiley symbol, are used to help let readers know that the writer is intending to be funny, happy, or lighthearted.

A whole host of emoticons have come into common usage, along with a long list of new symbolic terms like *l8r* for *later* and 2 for *to* or *too*. What symbols do you use on the computer?

1. What questions did you ask yourself before you read?
   _____
   _____

2. What questions did you ask yourself as you read?
   _____
   _____

3. How did the questions help you with the reading?
   _____
   _____

4. Does the smiley emoticon below have a line of symmetry? If so, draw it.

   :)

   _____

Fluency Tip
Be careful to read every word without skipping any words.

Reading Comprehension

READ on Your Own

Reading Comprehension Strategy: Metacognition

Ancient Cultures, pages 33–35

VOCABULARY

Watch for the words you are learning about.

hieroglyphics: a system of writing using pictures and symbols

symbolism: the use of signs or pictures to stand for other things

Fluency Tip

Reread sentences that you have trouble with. Rereading should help you read more smoothly.

Before You Read

Consider the tessellations in art that you read about in "In the Eyes of the Beholder." Why do you think this kind of pattern is used often to decorate homes and public buildings?

As You Read

Read "A Symbol Is Worth a Thousand Words," pages 33–35. STOP

Then answer the questions below.

Which strategies did you use to understand the pages?

_____
_____

How did these strategies help you understand the text?

_____
_____

How does choosing a strategy help you to better understand the text?

_____
_____

After You Read

What types of symbols might you choose to decorate your room? Explain your answer.

_____
_____

Problem Solving

SOLVE on Your Own

Ancient Cultures, page 36

Organize the Information

Read the Math Project in the magazine. Then use what you know about hieroglyphic symbols to fill in the table below. The first one has been done for you.

Number I Want to Show	Hieroglyphic Symbol
2	II
24	
130	

Math Project

Use the information from the Math Project to answer these questions. Write your answers in the space provided.

1. Do you think it was easier or more difficult to write and solve a math problem using Egyptian symbols? Explain.

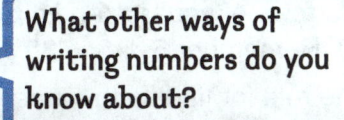

   _____
   _____

2. What problem-solving strategy would you suggest to someone trying to solve your problem?

   _____
   _____

What other ways of writing numbers do you know about?

After You Solve

What do you think are the main differences between hieroglyphic symbols and the numbers we use?

_____
_____
_____

Unit 7, Lesson 18   229

Connections

Put It Together

Introducing Justifying the Formula for the Area of a Rectangle

You have learned that you can find the area of a rectangle by counting the number of square units found within its perimeter on a coordinate graph. You have also used area models to explain multiplication. Both the coordinate graph model and the area models you use for multiplication will help you understand a formula (rule) you can use to find the area of a rectangle.

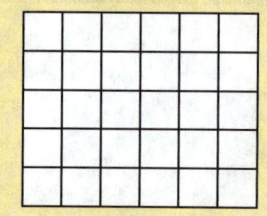

Does the model look familiar? It is the same model that was used to explain multiplication. There are five rows of squares and six columns of squares. The number of rows times the number of columns is 30. Remember $5 \times 6 = 30$ and $6 \times 5 = 30$.

The rule for finding the area of a rectangle is to multiply length by width. This rule can be written as a formula where A represents the area, l the length, and w the width.

So, the formula for finding the area of a rectangle is $A = l \times w$.

Practicing Justifying the Formula for the Area of a Rectangle

Use the formula $A = l \times w$ to find the area of each rectangle.

1. length 9 inches, width 7 inches _____

2. length 10 feet, width 9 feet _____

3. length 8 feet, width 7 feet _____

4. length 12 inches, width 24 inches _____

Unit 7, Lesson 19

YOUR TURN

Connections

Thinking About Justifying the Formula for the Area of a Rectangle

The area formula makes calculating the area of a rectangle quite simple. Follow these easy steps:

1. Write the formula.
2. Replace the letters with the known values.
3. Do the calculation.
4. Label your answer.
5. Check you work.

To find the area of a rectangle 17 yards long and 5 yards wide, replace the letters with the numbers and multiply.

$A = l \times w$
$A = 17 \text{ yd} \times 5 \text{ yd} = 85 \text{ yd}^2$

1. How does the rectangle formula help you compare the area of a rectangle with a length of 6 inches and a width of 9 inches to the area of a rectangle with a length of 9 inches and a width of 6 inches?

   _____

2. Why is it important to compare the unit of the measure of both length and width?

   _____
   _____

3. How could the formula help you find the width of a rectangle if you knew the area and length?

   _____

4. How can the formula help you explain that there is more than one rectangular shape that has an area of 18 square units?

   _____

Tip There are several different ways to write the area formula. "Base" and "height" are replaced by "length" and "width" in the formula used in this lesson.

Connections

Show That You Know

Read the information below. Use what you read about finding the area of a figure to answer the questions that follow. Remember what you have learned in this lesson about the formula for area. Use the space provided to show your work.

> The Parthenon is an ancient Greek temple built in the 5th century B.C. The building is about 110 feet wide and 250 feet long. Elana is building a model of the Parthenon for her history class project. Her model will be 11 inches wide and 25 inches long.

Formulas like the area formula make finding the answer easy. Plug in the numbers represented by each letter and solve.

1. What is the area of the model Parthenon that Elana is building? Show how you can use the formula to find the area of this rectangle.

2. What is the area of the Parthenon? Show how you can use the formula to find the area of this rectangle.

3. Compare the values you used in examples 1 and 2. How did the two formulas compare after you substituted in the values and before you did the calculation?

Unit 7, Lesson 19

Show That You Know (continued)

4. How were the Parthenon and the model measurements different?

5. After comparing the calculations, Elana said the area of the Parthenon is 100 times greater than the area of the model.

   Model: $A = l \times w$ Parthenon: $A = l \times w$

   $= 11 \times 25 = 110 \times 250$

   $= (10 \times 25) + (1 \times 25) = (10 \times 11) \times (10 \times 25) = (10 \times 10) \times (11 \times 25)$

   $= 275 = 100 \times 275$

   What is wrong with her conclusion?

Review What You've Learned

6. What have you learned in this Connections lesson about using a formula to find the area of a rectangle?

7. What have you learned in this Connections lesson that you did not already know?

8. What have you learned about formulas in this lesson that will help you use other formulas?

Review and Practice

Skills Review

Area of non-square polygons

The area of non-square and non-rectangle polygons can be estimated by superimposing a grid of square units on the figure and counting the squares.

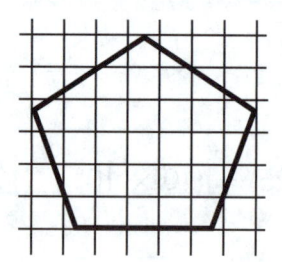

Estimating area

To estimate the area of a polygon, count the square units of a grid superimposed on the shape. Round partial units to the nearest half or whole number.

Area of triangles

Squares and rectangles decompose into two equal triangles.

The area of a triangle is half of the area of the rectangle.

Since the area of a rectangle $= b \times h$, the area of a triangle $= \frac{1}{2} \times (b \times h)$.

Area of other polygons

To find the area of a polygon with several sides, first decompose the polygon into squares, rectangles, and triangles. Find the area of each simple shape, and add these areas together to find the total area of the polygon.

Symmetry

A figure that has a line of symmetry will show symmetrical figures that are mirror images of one another along the line of symmetry.

Symmetrical figures that can be rotated to match one another have rotational symmetry.

Tessellations

A tessellation or tiling is made when a shape is copied several times and the copies are lined up side by side so that there are no gaps or overlaps.

Strategy Review

- When estimating the area of odd-shaped figures, find the area of a similarly-sized simple shape. The area of an odd shape can also be estimated by drawing the shape on graph paper.

- To find the area of shapes that are described in writing, first draw a picture of the shape and label its dimensions on the picture.

- Draw a picture or use models, such as cardboard cut-outs of shapes, to determine which shapes will make tessellations.

Review and Practice

Skills and Strategies Practice

Complete the exercises below.

1. Estimate the area of this triangle.

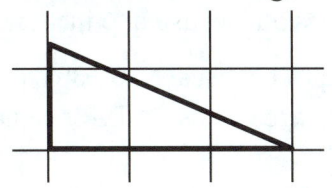

   _____

2. Estimate the area of a room that is 31.3 feet wide and 20.8 feet long.

   _____

3. What is the area of a triangle that has a height of 14 units and a base of 2 units?

   _____

4. A line is drawn through a long rectangle, from one corner to the opposite corner. What type of symmetry do the resulting triangles show?

   _____

5. What is the total area of four triangles whose bases are 11 cm and heights are 13 cm?

   _____

6. Why do semi-circles not make tessellations?

   _____
   _____
   _____

Test-Taking tip: When solving a math problem, remember to include the correct type of units in your answer. Area is always given in square units. A multiple choice question that asks you to give the area of a polygon may have answer choices with units of cm and answer choices with units of cm², for example. You know that cm is not correct for area, so you can cross out these answer choices.

Review and Practice

Unit Review

Circle the letter of the correct answer.

1. The estimated the area of this shape is _____.

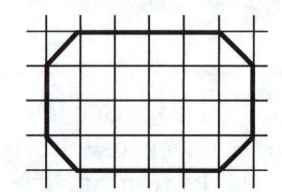

   A. 20 square units   C. 22 square units
   B. 21 square units   D. 24 square units

2. What is the area of a triangle that has a height of 2 feet and a base of 12 feet?

   A. 6 ft²   B. 24 ft²   C. 8 ft²   D. 12 ft²

3. A hexagon can be decomposed into six equal triangles, each with an area of 9 square inches. What is the area of the hexagon?

   A. 27 in.²   B. 15 in.²   C. 45 in.²   D. 54 in.²

4. Which of these creates figures with line symmetry?

   A. a line drawn from the top right to bottom left corner in a 3 × 3 square
   B. a line drawn from the top right corner to the bottom left corner in a 3 × 5 rectangle
   C. a line drawn from the top left corner to the bottom right corner in a 3 × 5 rectangle
   D. a line drawn at 1.9 units over from the top to bottom of a 3 × 3 square

5. The estimated the area of this trapezoid is _____ square units.

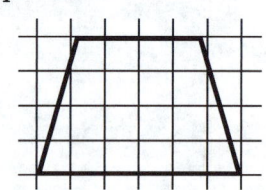

   A. 16   B. 20   C. 18   D. 24

6. Which of these shapes can form tessellations?

   A. hexagons   B. circles   C. hearts   D. stars

7. What is the area of a triangle that has a height of 5 inches and a base of 6 inches?

   A. 15 square inches   C. 30 square inches
   B. 11 square inches   D. 36 square inches

8. What is the area of a square with 2-inch sides?

   A. 2 in.²   B. 8 in.²   C. 4 in.²   D. 16 in.²

9. A hexagon can be decomposed into a rectangle with an area of 100 cm² and four equal triangles, each with an area of 5 cm². What is the area of the hexagon?

   A. 116 cm²   C. 120 cm²
   B. 112 cm²   D. 125 cm²

10. What is the area of this triangle?

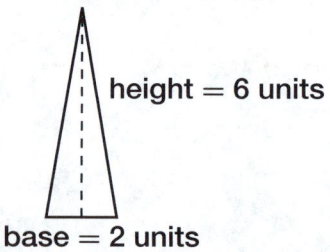

    height = 6 units
    base = 2 units

    A. 6 square units   C. 12 square units
    B. 8 square units   D. 10 square units

11. What is the estimated area of the non-shaded portion of this figure?

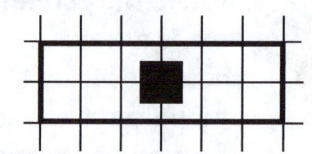

    A. 11 square units   C. 12 square units
    B. 10 square units   D. 9 square units

Review and Practice

12. Which of these cannot form tessellations?

A. circle   C. square
B. hexagon   D. right triangle

13. Which line is a line of symmetry?

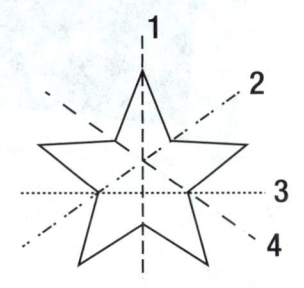

A. 2   B. 1   C. 4   D. 3

14. What is the area of a triangle that has a base of 11 cm and a height of 4 cm?

A. 22 cm   B. 22 cm²   C. 44 cm   D. 44 cm²

15. A shape is composed of two squares, each with 4 cm long sides. What is the area of this shape?

A. 16 cm²   B. 24 cm²   C. 32 cm²   D. 40 cm²

16. A shape is composed of a triangle and a square. The square has 5 cm long sides and the triangle has a 2 cm base and height of 1 cm. What is the area of this shape?

A. 26.5 square cm   C. 25 square cm
B. 27 square cm   D. 26 square cm

17. What is the area of this figure?

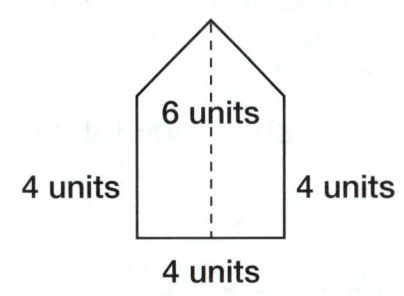

6 units
4 units   4 units
4 units

A. 16 units²   C. 24 units²
B. 20 units²   D. 22 units²

18. What is the area of a triangle that has a base of 40 meters and a height of 20 meters?

A. 200 m²   C. 400 m²
B. 800 m²   D. 80 m²

19. What is the area of a rectangle that measures 8 feet by 11 feet?

A. 88 ft²   C. 86 ft²
B. 44 ft²   D. 44 ft

20. The estimated area of this figure is _____.

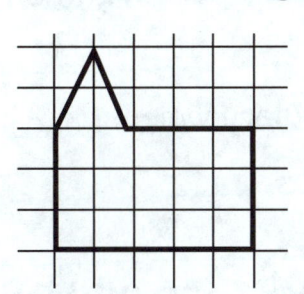

A. 16 square units
B. 19 square units
C. 15 square units
D. 17 square units

Unit 7, Lesson 20   237

Unit 7 Reflection

MATH SKILLS

The easiest part about finding area is

A coordinate grid is useful because

MATH STRATEGIES & CONNECTIONS

For me, the math strategies that work the best are

Using models to find area is like using the formulas because

READING STRATEGIES & COMPREHENSION

The easiest part about metacognition is

One way that metacognition helps me with reading is

The vocabulary words I had trouble with are

INDEPENDENT READING

My favorite part of Ancient Cultures is

I read most fluently when

Ancient Cultures

GLOSSARY

UNITS 5-7

A

acute angle (uh-KYOOT ANG-gul): an angle with a measure between 0° and 90° (p. 91)

acute triangle (uh-KYOOT TRY-ang-gul): a triangle with all angles measuring less than 90° (p. 128)

angle (ANG-gul): formed by two rays with a common endpoint called the vertex (p. 91)

area (EHR-ee-uh): the number of square units enclosed by a region (p. 164)

B

base (bays): the number used as a factor in an expression with an exponent (p. 59); a side of a polygon; length (p. 164)

C

combined shapes (kum-BYND shayps): shapes that are made of two or more polygons (p. 121)

complementary angles (kahm-pluh-MEN-tuh-ree ANG-gulz): two angles for which the sum of their measures is 90° (p. 128)

congruent (kahn-GROO-unt): exactly equal (p. 84)

cube (kyoob): a number raised to the third power (p. 59)

D

decompose (dee-kum-POHZ): to break apart a shape into other shapes (p. 121)

divisible (duh-VIZ-uh-bul): able to be divided evenly by another number (p. 11)

E

equilateral triangle (ee-kwih-LAT-ur-ul TRY-ang-gul): a triangle with three congruent sides (p. 102)

exponent (ek-SPOHN-unt): a number that tells how many times a base is used as a factor; also called a power (p. 59)

F

formula (FAWR-myoo-luh): symbols that make a mathematical statement (p. 208)

H

height (hyt): the distance from top to bottom; width (p. 164)

I

interval (IN-tur-vul): the space or time between things (p. 22)

isosceles triangle (eye-SAHS-uh-leez TRY-ang-gul): a triangle with at least two congruent sides (p. 102)

L

line of symmetry (lyn uv SIM-uh-tree): a line that divides a figure into mirror images (p. 139)

M

multidigit number (mul-tee-DIJ-it NUM-bur): a number with more than one digit (p. 22)

O

obtuse angle (ahb-TOOS ANG-gul): an angle with a measure greater than 90° and less than 180° (p. 91)

obtuse triangle (ahb-TOOS TRY-ang-gul): a triangle with one obtuse angle (p. 128)

overestimate (oh-vur-ES-tuh-mayt): to round up; to guess more than you think your answer will be (p. 25)

GLOSSARY continued

P

parallelogram (pa-ruh-LEL-uh-gram): a quadrilateral with both pairs of opposite sides parallel (p. 102)

partial product (PAHR-shul PRAHD-ukt): the product of a number and one digit of a multidigit number (p. 41)

partial unit (PAHR-shul YOO-nit): a part of a whole unit (p. 201)

polygon (PAHL-ih-gahn): a closed figure that is formed by three or more line segments that do not cross (p. 84)

Q

quadrilateral (kwah-drih-LAT-ur-ul): a polygon with four sides (p. 84)

R

ray (ray): a part of a line, beginning at an endpoint and continuing in one direction with no end (p. 91)

rectangle (REK-tang-gul): a parallelogram with four right angles (p. 102)

regroup (ree-GROOP): to form into a new grouping; for example, 10 ones become 1 ten and 10 tens become one hundred (p. 41)

regular polygon (REG-yuh-lur PAHL-ih-gahn): a polygon with all angles and sides congruent (p. 84)

rhombus (RAHM-bus): a parallelogram with four congruent sides (p. 102)

right angle (ryt ANG-gul): an angle with a measure of 90° (p. 91)

right triangle (ryt TRY-ang-gul): a triangle with one angle measuring 90° (p. 128)

rotation (roh-TAY-shun): a transformation that turns a figure about a fixed center point (p. 121)

rotational symmetry (roh-TAY-shun-ul SIM-uh-tree): rotation that shows congruence (p. 219)

S

scalene triangle (SKAY-leen TRY-ang-gul): a triangle with no congruent sides (p. 102)

square (skwehr): a number raised to the second power (p. 59); a quadrilateral with four right angles and four congruent sides (p. 102)

square unit (skwehr YOO-nit): a square with sides 1 unit long used to measure area (p. 171)

straight angle (strayt ANG-gul): an angle with a measure of 180° (p. 91)

superimpose (SOO-pur-im-pohz): to lay or place on top of something else (p. 201)

supplementary angles (sup-luh-MEN-tur-ee ANG-gulz): two angles for which the sum of their measures is 180° (p. 128)

symmetry (SIM-uh-tree): a figure has symmetry if it can be folded along a line so both parts match exactly (p. 139)

T

tessellation (tes-uh-LAY-shun): when one or more shapes is repeated over and over again fitting together without any overlap or gaps (p. 219)

tiling (tyl-ING): another word for tessellation (p. 219)

transformation (trans-fur-MAY-shun): a change in the position, shape, or size of a figure (p. 121)

translation (trans-LAY-shun): a transformation that slides each point of a figure the same distance and in the same direction (p. 121)

trapezoid (TRAP-ih-zoyd): a quadrilateral with one pair of opposite sides parallel (p. 102)

triangle (TRY-ang-gul): a polygon with three sides (p. 84)

U

underestimate (un-dur-ES-tuh-mayt): to round down; to guess less than you think your answer will be (p. 25)

unit (YOO-nit): one of the parts into which a whole can be analyzed (p. 164)

unit square (YOO-nit skwehr): a square with sides that are 1 unit in length and having an area of 1 square unit (p. 164)

V

vertex (VUR-teks): the point at which two sides of an angle meet (p. 91)

STAFF CREDITS

Josh Adams, Amanda Aranowski, Mel Benzinger, Karen Blonigen, Carol Bowling, Sarah Brandel, Kazuko Collins, Nancy Condon, Barb Drewlo, Sue Gulsvig, Daren Hastings, Laura Henrichsen, Ruby Hogen-Chin, Becky Johnson, Julie Johnston, Jody Manderfeld, Carol Nelson, Heather Oakley-Thompson, Carrie O'Connor, Deb Rogstad, Marie Schaefle, Julie Theisen, LeAnn Velde, Mike Vineski, Peggy Vlahos, Charmaine Whitman, Sue Will

PHOTO AND ILLUSTRATION CREDITS

Cover: background, © Brand X Pictures; top right, © Shutterstock; bottom, © Glenn Walker/Shutterstock; p. 1: background, © Jack Hollingsworth/Stockbyte/Getty Images; foreground, © Brand X Pictures; p. 2, © Pattie Steib/Shutterstock; p. 19, © Christophe Testi/Shutterstock; p. 30, © Natalia Bratslavsky/Shutterstock; p. 35, © Christian Sawicki/iStockphoto; p. 66, © Brand X Pictures; p. 67, NASA; p. 72, © Rzymu/Shutterstock; p. 78: top, © Brand X Pictures; bottom, © JuiceDrops; p. 79: background © Jack Hollingsworth/Stockbyte/Getty Images; foreground, © Glenn Walker/Shutterstock; p. 80, © Glenn Walker/Shutterstock; p. 99, © fat_fa_tin/Shutterstock; p. 110, © Dan Collier/Shutterstock; p. 115, © JuiceDrops; p. 147, © Mary Terriberry/Shutterstock; p. 158: top, © Glenn Walker/Shutterstock; bottom, © JuiceDrops; p. 159: background, © Jack Hollingsworth/Stockbyte/Getty Images; foreground, © Shutterstock; p. 161, © Alfredo Schaufelberger/Shutterstock; p. 179, © Chris Howey/Shutterstock; p. 216, © Kutlayev Dmitry/Shutterstock; p. 232, © polartern/Shutterstock; p. 238: top, © Shutterstock; bottom, © JuiceDrops; Back Cover: top, © Brand X Pictures; middle, © Glenn Walker/Shutterstock; bottom, © Shutterstock

All coach characters: KATMO